Rediscover Alaska

"An eloquent, heartfelt summing-up of one American life—and a treasure for today's readers in the lower forty-eight . . . guaranteed to make readers wish they'd been there at his side."

—Kirkus Reviews

"I like *North of the Sun* for its account of life in a pristine country, and also for its economy and clarity. Mr. Hatfield knows how to tell a story, and he doesn't fool around."

—Wendell Berry

"Engaging . . . captivating . . . a fine piece of nostalgia, a picture of camaraderie and pioneering at a time when Alaska was the frontier."

—Publishers weekly

"Looking back on his Alaska days from the perspective of eighty years, Hatfield writes with a simple elegance absent a young writer's affectations. . . . Alaska literature is not rich in memoirs of the quality of *North of the Sun*."

—Anchorage Daily News

"A real-life American hero—strong, silent, skillful— steps out of the pages of this adventure. . . . Hatfield's spare prose does justice to the beauty and drama of Alaskan life."

—-Booklist

North of

A Memoir of the

❊ ❊ ❊ ❊ ❊

A Citadel Press Book

the Sun

Alaskan Wilderness

FRED HATFIELD

Published by Carol Publishing Group

For Ann

First paperback edition 1992

A Citadel Press Book
Published by Carol Publishing Group
Citadel Press is a registered trademark of Carol Communications, Inc.

Editorial Offices: 600 Madison Avenue, New York, N.Y. 10022
Sales & Distribution Offices: 120 Enterprise Avenue, Secaucus, N.J. 07094
In Canada: Canadian Manda Group, P.O. Box 920, Station U, Toronto,
    Ontario M8Z 5P9

Queries regarding rights and permissions should be addressed to Carol Publishing Group, 600 Madison Avenue, New York, N.Y. 10022

Carol Publishing Group books are available at special discounts for bulk purchases, for sales promotions, fund raising, or educational purposes. Special editions can be created to specifications. For details contact: Special Sales Department, Carol Publishing Group, 120 Enterprise Avenue, Secaucus, N.J. 07094

Manufactured in the United States of America
10   9   8   7   6   5   4   3   2   1

Library of Congress Cataloging-in-Publication Data

North of the sun : a memoir of the Alaskan wilderness / Fred
Hatfield.
     p.   cm.

1. Hatfield, Fred, 1910-   . 2. Frontier and pioneer life--
Alaska. 3. Alaska--Social life and customs. 4. Pioneers--Alaska--
Biography. 5. Alaska--Biography. I. Title.
F908.H37   1990
979.8'04'092--dc20   90-42593
[B]   CIP

Contents

Author's Note   vii
Map   viii

1 / Alaska: The Great Land   3
2 / Togiak   14
3 / The Bering Sea Coast   30
4 / Klutuk   46
5 / John Shipton   73
6 / 1939   89
7 / Ann   105
8 / War in the Wilderness   136
9 / Changes   153
10 / Earthquake and Moose Murder   162
11 / A Lonely Time   171
12 / The Big Lake Country   178

Author's Note

THE ACCOUNT OF JOHN SHIPTON in 1938 is set down here exactly the way it occurred and is faithful in every detail except one. In order to shield his family I have given him a surname not his own.

In the history of the Second World War, I have been able to find little about the Battle of Attu. The only record I have found is brief and confined to military matters:

"On June 14, 1942, Japanese garrisons arrived by sea to seize and occupy the islands of Kiska, Attu and Agattu in Alaska's Aleutian chain. The only part of North America invaded in the war, it remained in enemy hands until, on May 11, 1943, American and Canadian troops, numbering 100,000 men, landed on Attu and annihilated the 2,350 Japanese defenders in a particularly savage campaign. Three months later the Japanese evacuated Kiska and withdrew from the Aleutians."

It has often seemed strange to me that there has never been any mention of the people who lived on Attu, or their savage and senseless death, or other fate, at the hands of the Japanese. It is almost as though they never existed.

F.H., 1990

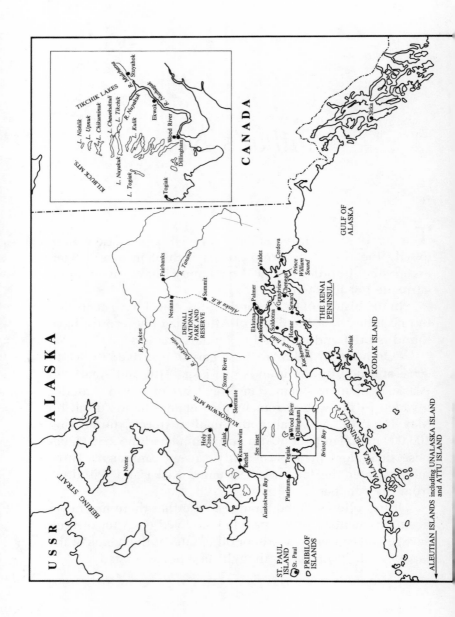

North of the Sun

1 / *Alaska: The Great Land*

IT WAS IN THE MONTH OF DECEMBER. The nights were long and cold and daybreak didn't show until about nine o'clock. At the first sign of light I stepped outside the cabin and then I heard it: a sound rolling down from the high mountains.

It was music, the tones beautiful and changing as though a huge bank of organs, somewhere, had proclaimed the coming of a new day. The sound finally died away, and it was over. I believe the heat from the rising sun met the cold from the frigid mountains, and nature did the rest.

It must have been forty degrees below zero that morning, and I returned to the warmth of my cabin. I had lived alone in this big valley for five years and nature had taught me many things, yet I never ceased to wonder about the mystery and greatness of it all. Or perhaps, as the old Eskimo Peetla had told me, it was just that this valley was the place of the gods.

* * *

I was born in the State of Maine and I don't believe there's a better place in the world for a boy to grow up. There was always plenty of trout fishing and when I got old enough I went deer hunting in the fall.

The end of high school and the great Depression arrived at the same time. I finally found a job. The pay was twenty-five cents an hour, ten hours a day, six days a week. I worked and saved what I could. Any more school for me was out of the question, and by the spring of 1933 I was ready for what I had in mind.

The great cry, "Go west, young man, go west," had died long before, but there was one place left that had plenty of room for people. I had always done a lot of reading and was fascinated with what I had learned about Alaska: the tremendous rivers, the wide, deep valleys filled with game, the mountains, the space. Everything about it seemed just fine.

One day that spring my mother and father hugged me goodbye. My mother told me to be careful and my dad said if he was ten years younger, he'd go with me. I didn't know it then, but it would be many long years before I ever saw any of my family again. I rode the train to New York, got off at Grand Central Station and left the same day on the Greyhound bus for Seattle.

The Alaskan Steamship Line was, at that time, the only possible way to travel to Alaska. When I arrived in Seattle I went down to the dock at once and tried for a job as a deck hand, but too many men had the same idea and I didn't make it. Instead, I bought a steerage ticket for Seward, at the southern end of the Alaska Railroad.

We left the next day and, after a hundred miles or so, entered the series of connecting straits and passages which form the coastline of British Columbia. For two days we passed along a solid range of mountains sloping sharply to the water's edge. The peaks reached into the sky, some of them hidden by clouds. The steep, lower hills were dotted here and there with snow-white mountain sheep and goats. In some places you could have thrown a rock to shore; the outer side of the passage was a series of interlocking islands. Porpoises and seals were everywhere, the porpoises at times racing alongside the ship, crossing over in front of the bow. For them it was a game, and they were a pleasure to watch.

We arrived in Seward on the sixth day. A crowd of longshoremen was on the dock, ready to unload the cargo. Deckhands on board threw heavy lines over the side and in a short time the ship was tied up and made fast, the gangplank lowered. After the first-class passengers were ashore it was our turn, the men who rode steerage.

Seward was a small town, nestled at the foot of high mountains, facing Resurrection Bay. The steamship company had a small office on the dock. I carried my suitcase inside and left it with the clerk. The dock was connected with the shore by a short bridge. I crossed that and went on up the sidewalk and it didn't take long to walk the length of the main street: two stores, a bank, a restaurant and a small rooming house. There was one building set off the main street with a sign on it: "Seward Fire Dept." Under that it read: "Seward Police Dept." I walked over to the door, marked "Office," opened it and went in. The man sitting at the desk was big, but there was no fat on him. He looked at me for a few seconds.

"You wanted to see me?"

"I'm looking for work."

He shook his head. "You're a little early for work around here. Most of the men that come in on the boat keep on going north."

"I can't get very far on the money I've got."

"We're going to build a boat harbor here this summer. You'll find work then. Where are you from?"

I told him.

"You came a long way. Listen, I've got a small cabin down on the beach. You can have it for five dollars a month."

"I'll take it." I pulled out my wallet and started to count out the money.

"You'd better put that in your pocket. You can pay me after you find work. Just wait here a minute."

He got to his feet and went out. I could hear him going up a stairway on the outside of the building. When he came back he was carrying a box.

"My wife canned some salmon, moose meat and other things. I'll be right back."

When he came down again he had another filled box. He set it down and held out his hand.

"I'm Fred Kilcheski. I'm the police chief and the police force. I'm also the fire chief. We have a volunteer department here. Let's take these boxes, there's a pickup outside."

We drove down the street to the edge of town, then down across the beach. The cabin had a windbreak built on the front and as we went through I noticed a sawhorse with a bucksaw leaning against it. The kitchen was neat, with a wood stove and plates, pots and pans stacked in place on shelves. The bedroom had a small bed on each side, with blankets and pillows.

"There are some fish lines out in the windbreak. If you fish off the dock you can catch all the rock cod you can eat and once in a while a halibut. If you need anything, come and see me."

That was long ago and Fred Kilcheski has gone where all good men go. He was one of the kindest men I have ever known.

❄ ❄ ❄

I had been in Seward about three weeks when I saw a sign in the Bank of Seward window: Jackhammer Men Wanted. I went inside and walked to the girl sitting at a desk. I said I could run a jackhammer and was looking for work. She told me to walk down the road leading out of town and I'd find the job they had under way before I went very far. She gave me a piece of paper with a man's name on it and told me to ask for him. The job consisted of drilling a tunnel into the base of a huge rock cliff for about seventy yards, then drilling cross-cuts about thirty yards each way. These would be loaded with cases of dynamite, and after the face of the mountain was blown down there would be enough broken rock to construct the boat harbor the town needed. It didn't take the boss long to tell me what to do but it turned out to be the hardest work I ever did in my life. The job ran twenty-four hours a day and my shift went to work at six o'clock in the evening. The tunnel was four and a half feet high and when we forgot and stood up too straight, the hide was raked off our backs again and again. Still, it paid a dollar an hour and that was big money for the Depression years.

The job took almost four months and then the big day arrived. I went to the top of the cliff with the foreman, moving plenty far back to be out of the way. We had an electric detonator with us, connected to the hundreds of cases of powder packed into the tunnels. Watching the town's highway, we saw the men stationed there to keep back traffic give the all-clear signal. The boss pushed down the handle of the detonator and the whole rock face collapsed. Before winter set in, Seward had its boat harbor. My work was over for the year and I had more money than I had ever seen.

❄ ❄ ❄

It was late fall and cool enough for meat to keep. I wasn't a resident of Alaska yet and a non-resident hunting license cost more than I wanted to spend, so I talked with the area game warden and asked him what would happen if I went out and tried to get a little meat for the winter. All he asked was how long I had been in Seward and if I planned to spend the winter there. I told him what he wanted to know, and he said no one would bother me.

All summer long the Alaska Railroad had crews of men at work, keeping the tracks in good shape, with a section house every ten miles for their living quarters. This was over now, but each section house kept a man on the job all winter.

Sixty miles out of Seward was a place called Grandview. A section house was there and I knew a winter man would be too. I already had a .22 and a .30–40 Krag rifle which weighed almost ten pounds. I bought a packboard and a few things I needed, then boarded the train. It was a convenient way to travel: the conductor would stop the train to let a passenger on or off anywhere along the line. I got off at Grandview.

It was beautiful country, with long mountain slopes that started from where I stood and seemed to go up and up forever until they were lost in the high, distant peaks. I walked to the section house door and knocked. The door opened and a man stood there, staring at me. He looked to be in his sixties.

"You may as well come in."

I walked inside.

"Put your things down and pull up a chair. You want a cup of coffee?"

"Thanks, I sure do."

I put my pack on the floor, laid my rifles against it and sat down at the table. He brought my coffee and sat it down in front of me.

"I see you plan to go hunting."

I started to tell him but he raised his hand.

"Just a minute. Do you know you're in a game-protected area?"

"No, I didn't know that."

"Well, you are. You're in the Chugach Game Reserve. That means no hunting."

He walked to my Krag and picked it up. It may have been a relic of the Boer War but it was accurate enough.

"Son, how old are you?"

"I'm twenty-four."

He nodded his head and said, "This gun is older than you are. Where did you get it?"

"I bought it from a guy on the dock in Seward who was going back to the States."

He put the rifle down, got a cup of coffee for himself, then sat across the table from me.

"You still plan to hunt in these hills?"

"Well, I don't think one goat would hurt anything."

"No," he said. "One goat won't hurt anything, but suppose everyone thought the same way?"

I told him I didn't think anyone else would hunt in here.

"You know, I believe you're right. I don't think anyone else would be such a damn fool. And I'll tell you something else. You're welcome to stay here for one reason—because I don't get much company—but I'll have nothing to do with your hunting."

That seemed to be all he wanted to tell me and we spent the evening together and it was pleasant enough. His name was Mack Danby and he had been the section foreman at Grandview ever since they put the railroad through.

The next morning was crisp and clear. I crossed the tracks and climbed a steep slope that finally leveled off into a plateau. It was easy walking and as I moved on I could feel the mountain country settling on me like comfortable old clothes. I walked round a bend and not a hundred yards away saw a male goat and a smaller female, lying at the base of a large boulder. It wasn't a difficult shot and I got them both. As I was going to have to drag them down to the section house, I left the hides on but I cleaned them both and removed the heads. The male had a beautiful set of horns and I wanted to keep them. I left the horns where they were so that I could pick them up the next day, and started back. Most of the way home was downhill and it wasn't too hard getting both goats down to the railroad track. I took the male with me and hustled across, leaving the female in the brush.

The old foreman spotted me and told me to get my damn goat behind the building. I did as he told me and then I was in a little bit of a quandary. The other goat was for him and I hesitated to say so. Finally I decided that the truth was best.

"Mack, I've got a goat for you. It's on the other side of the tracks."

He stared at the ground for what seemed like an hour, but it couldn't have been more than a few seconds. When he spoke his voice was hoarse.

"Go get it and hurry!"

We hung the carcasses from a timber behind the building and both started to skin them. I don't think he stopped a steady, muttering tirade until we finished. He had a meat house that was used for the summer work crew, and we hung our meat in there. The walls were double and thick and would keep it cool. Still hurrying, Mack came to me with a shovel and told me to dig a hole deep enough to bury the hides. Afterwards he fixed a nice supper for us and we sat around talking. He had cooled off quite a lot and had plenty to tell me. He had been in Alaska a long time. I suppose he had come there about the time I was born.

I had seen a flock of snow-white ptarmigan on the higher slopes and, the next morning promising another fine day, I set out again with my .22. It didn't take me long to reach the spot where I had left the goat horns, but they were gone. Looking round, I saw a scattered piece of entrail here and there leading up a steep slope. As I looked, a large brown head raised itself over the top of the slope. It was a grizzly bear, the first I had ever seen, and he had my goat horns.

I had read about grizzlies and knew they commanded a lot of respect, but I hated to let this one have my horns. I walked up the slope carrying my .22 in one hand and waving the other, shouting and hoping to scare him off. That I did. The huge head disappeared and as I reached the top of the slope he was gone. Right in front of me was the remnant of an old glacier, a field of ice, full of crevices and ice caverns. I stooped to pick up my horns and then I heard a sound so horrifying it seemed the sky had fallen. It came from under a large, overhanging ice shelf. The grizzly wasn't more than ten yards away and he was coming fast. His size was unbelievable. His huge mouth was wide open and his roar of rage made the mountains tremble.

The slope I had climbed was rough and full of jagged rocks but I had no trouble reaching the bottom of it and I kept on going. The roaring didn't stop but I seemed to be leaving it behind and I realized he wasn't in pursuit. I stopped long enough to take a look back and saw him still on the crest of the slope, moving his tremendous weight from one foot to the other, undecided about coming after me. As I watched he turned and disappeared.

My right hand felt painful and I looked down at it. The knuckles were white from the hard grasp I had round one of the goat horns. I had forgotten I had them.

I didn't stick around long—all thoughts of ptarmigan were forgotten and I hurried toward the haven of the section house. On my way down the mountain I followed a bend round a clifftop that rose straight up with perhaps twenty feet of flat ground between its base and another sheer drop. As I rounded the bend I came face to face with a band of at least thirty goats coming my way. I stood still and they parted in the center and passed me by. They were all sizes, big ones, little ones and in between. They didn't hurry their sedate pace. I could have touched a wild mountain goat with either hand. If they had panicked, many of them would have been forced over the drop. Goats are difficult to stalk and I have only one explanation: this encounter was so unexpected, so complete and final, that they simply accepted me as part of the mountain. I was happy for them as they passed safely.

I arrived at the section house a wiser man than when I left that morning. I had learned two valuable lessons. One, never try to bluff a grizzly and two, never travel grizzly country with just a .22 rifle.

I stayed overnight again with Mack and the next morning he flagged down the train for me.

"Fred, this winter you could jump on the train and come spend a few days with me. It gets kind of lonely sometimes."

"I will, Mack, you can depend on it."

I went out to Grandview three times that winter. Mack was a fine old man.

✳ ✳ ✳

There was a trading store in Seward, called Cowen and Hawkins. A few of the old-timers who had been in on the Nome and Klondike gold strikes had settled here. I got to know them and spent a lot of time with them that winter, trying to find out what I could about prospecting for gold. They all had stories of the old days, most of them about how they had almost struck it rich. One thing they agreed on was that old man Cowen, of Cowen and Hawkins, had been a member of Soapy Smith's gang in Sitka. I used to look at him and wonder what thoughts might drift through his mind when he remembered his days with Soapy.

Smith had been the leader of a vicious gang. Any man who came out of the hills with even a small poke of gold stood a good chance of being found dead in some back alley or along the waterfront. Frank Reed was mayor of Sitka at that time and also editor of the local paper. Crime reached such a level in the town that he decided to take justice into his own hands. He loaded his rifle and went looking for Soapy. He found him on the dock by the waterfront and told him to leave town or he'd be placed under arrest. Smith pulled his revolver, Reed leveled his rifle, and both men fired. Smith died at once, Frank Reed two days later.

Cowen always wore a nice suit now and had a pure white handlebar mustache. He was a distinguished-looking old gent. Maybe in his younger days he had just been one of the wild ones. It was 1934 now, and all this had happened thirty-six years before my time in Alaska.

2 / *Togiak*

Sometimes a small thing will change the course of our lives. I bought the Anchorage paper only once that winter and an article I read in it surely changed the course of mine.

A reindeer herder had brought a large gold nugget into the small village of Dillingham in the dead of winter. He said he had found it at the head of Togiak Lake in an open creek, one that was fed by warm springs and didn't freeze over. The more I thought about it, the bigger that nugget seemed to grow. I bought a map of Alaska. Dillingham was far to the west on the Bering Sea coast and Togiak Lake was roughly west of there, and inland perhaps seventy miles. The story kept running through my head like a half-remembered song. I knew where I was going to be the following summer.

Spring finally arrived and my mind was still on Togiak and gold. I boarded the train for Anchorage one day and was on my way; the train passed Grandview and I wondered how Mack was making out. Finally we reached a place called Summit where the grade was so steep that even with two engines pulling we had to stop at the bottom and everyone had to get off and walk behind the train. At the top of Summit we climbed back aboard.

Anchorage at that time wasn't a big town: Fourth Avenue was the one main street. In all of Alaska then, even though all distant travel was by air, there were fewer than seventy commercial aircraft scattered over the entire Territory, and most of those were small bush planes. Star Airways had an office on Fourth Avenue. I went there and told them where I wanted to go and learned that a pilot would be showing up soon who could fly me to Dillingham.

I hung around the office most of the time but I had plenty of leisure to look the town over. One thing puzzled me. In the restaurant windows there were signs: No Natives Allowed or No Natives Wanted. It puzzled me because in Seward I had known many native people. I had been in their homes and they were my friends. There had been no signs in the restaurants there. I didn't like what I saw in Anchorage.

❄ ❄ ❄

On the third day my pilot arrived. We left Anchorage next morning and set down in Dillingham that afternoon. It was small, just a fishing village at the mouth of the Nushagak River. I bought my supplies at the trading store and wished I had a little more money; the plane fare had made quite a hole in my pocket.

Togiak Lake was about seventy miles northwest of Dillingham, an hour's flying time the next morning. We landed at the mouth of a river flowing into the lake and unloaded my supplies. The pilot told me that when I wanted to get out I could follow the lake, fifteen miles of it, then follow the river that emptied out of it. About ninety miles would put me on the coast of the Bering Sea. He gunned his engine and the plane was out of sight in minutes. I stared at the mountain pass where I had last seen him and it was then that I realized I was finally out in the wilderness.

The Togiak valley was not more than five miles wide. A mountain range running north to south formed the west side, with the same type of range laid to the east. Twenty miles north of me they joined together, forming an almost up-and-down jagged barrier. South was the lake, of course, and beyond that what looked like an unlimited stretch of nothing extending to an empty horizon. To either side of this, in the far distance, were the tops of two mountain peaks. I had an idea they marked the end of the mountain ranges and that the Bering Sea couldn't be far beyond.

Locating a cabin site was my first job and it was an unpleasant surprise to find that the pilot had landed me on the wrong side of the river: north as far as I could see there was nothing but alder brush. I was too far west for any spruce timber, but on the other side of the river a nice stand of cottonwood extended for a long way. The lake shore was littered with dry drift logs and it didn't take me long to tie a raft together, load my supplies and paddle around the river mouth to the other side. Walking ashore, I eventually found a flat area that looked as though it had never been under water and decided to build there. I had a small tarpaulin to hang for a temporary shelter and I started back to the lake shore to get it. A coughing grunt and a crash in the brush took my mind off that and I hustled instead for my rifle. I came back and after a slow, careful stalk found the tracks of a black bear. That didn't pose any problem. Black bears are quite shy and peaceful unless they are disturbed when their young are with them, and I knew this was too far west to be grizzly country.

I made my cabin ten feet square: I didn't need much room. I covered the roof logs with a thick layer of moss and over that put a layer of sod to hold everything in place. I had forgotten that a small pane of glass would be nice for a window. I had also forgotten that a good supply of candles could make things a little more cheerful at night. Still, there were plenty of porcupine around at that time of year and I cooked the fat from those. The result was a thick soupy grease that gave off a red flame. There wasn't much light but it sure produced plenty of black smoke.

The lake and streams were alive with trout. Mallard and teal were everywhere. I lived like a king and was eager to see what my country was like. One day I left the cabin, headed north and found a game trail close to the mountains. It was a good eight feet wide and at one time had been a migration route for caribou. Small trees about four inches in diameter were growing across it now, showing that it hadn't been used by game for a long time. The settlement of a number of people on the Kuskokwim River to the west had been too much for them.

Ten miles up the valley I came to a low pass opening from the west. The game trail turned into it and so did I. All that day there was nothing to see except a good-sized creek far below me; it followed the pass and emptied into the river, north of my cabin. I made camp that night in a small canyon, grateful for the shelter it gave me from the wind that never seemed to stop blowing. There was dry cottonwood in the bottom for a fire.

The next day I came to a high rise and stopped to look around. There was nothing that looked like gold country, but on the far side of the creek I could see a small herd of reindeer. I knew them for reindeer because of the color variations; some of them were black and white, some were brown, and they were being herded by a pearl-white bull. I traveled down the slope and crossed the creek with no trouble. Reindeer are almost a domesticated animal and I had no difficulty getting within easy range. I shot the white bull and a small black calf. I wanted the thin hide of the calf for a window—fleshed well on both sides, it would be almost transparent. The rest of the herd moved off westwards; they had strayed from a much larger herd somewhere on the Kuskokwim and now they were headed back.

I dressed my meat and carried it all down to the creek bottom, where I made camp. I was lucky to have the tarpaulin: it rained day and night for five days. The meat soured and except for what I had eaten, I lost all of it. The creek had swollen from the long rain and if I wanted to get across and back on to the caribou trail I knew I was going to get wet. I kept my boots on but removed all my clothing and tied it on top of the pack and started straight across. About ten feet from shore the water boiled up around my chest and I felt my boots slipping on the smooth stones in the creek bottom. About twenty yards behind me it entered a canyon with sheer rock walls fifty feet high. I knew if I went into that I'd never come out. Fighting the current and wrestling with the pack, I made my feet slide sideways as the water forced me backwards and slowly I made knee-deep water and got back more or less to where I'd started.

I walked up the shoreline, looking for a wider, shallower place to cross, and at the mouth of a small side creek a small cabin showed ahead of me. It had been there a long time: the roof poles were still in place but all the moss and sod were gone. I walked inside. It was bare, with nothing to show that anyone had ever lived there. I didn't realize it at the time, but whoever built that cabin had worked there, and there was only one kind of work in that pass. A man had lived there and mined the small creek.

I was twenty-four years old and I must have been stupid. I had come into this country looking for gold and why I didn't check that creek, I'll never know. Instead I kept on going and finally came to a wide shallow spot where a creek came in from the other side and I could wade across with no trouble. There was an odd formation a short way up the creek: a dike or ridge had been cut through by the water and there was a small growth of cottonwood, enough for a shelter and wood for a fire to dry my boots and socks. As I pulled my clothes on I noticed plenty of quartz in the creek and dug the gold pan out of my pack. The very first pan of gravel gave me fairly coarse placer gold and a nugget the size of a small marble. During the rest of the day I took eight ounces of gold from the top of the gravel bar.

That evening I had oatmeal for supper. It had become damp during the long rain and didn't taste too good. Tired, I remembered I had a fish line in my pack and as it was still light enough I tried the main creek for trout. There was nothing. I bedded down for the night and in the morning tried several other places for fish and finally knew there were none.

I was on a good, paying creek, though, and I knew that. I had thought that finding gold would be the difficult thing but it hadn't turned out that way: my gold was in a hungry place and working that creek would be the problem. The need to find food had moved into first place. There was no game in the pass and the reindeer I had seen were well on their way back to where they came from. I had no choice so I broke camp and headed back to the lake. I would have to get the right kind of food to take in to the creek, food that would keep and not turn sour from damp weather. It meant a tent and a small Yukon stove. I would have to make the money to pay for them by trapping. Perhaps it would work out for me next year.

When I saw a glimpse of my cabin through the cotton-woods it looked like home. Salmon were beginning to show up in the streams ready to spawn, and soon they were so plentiful I could flip them out of the water with a stick. I worked on the calf hide for my window, scraping every trace of flesh away. Then I tied a rope to it, threw it out into the lake and made the end fast. After five days of soaking I pulled the skin from the water and wiped off all the hair. Scraping the hair side with my knife, I soon had it thin and almost transparent. I cut a square opening in my cabin wall and tacked the hide in place. It let in plenty of light.

I had never seen what the lower end of the lake looked like and decided to make myself a new raft, complete with crude oarlocks. On a fine clear morning I set out to have a look. It took me some time to make the fifteen miles, but the raft worked well. Just before I reached the lake's end I spotted a large brown animal on the tundra. I couldn't make out what it was so I beached my raft and made my way up the slope; all of it was small ridges with shallow dips in between. Ridge after ridge was the same. Nothing in sight. I had one fervent hope, that I wasn't stalking a grizzly, not like this.

I eased to the top of a ridge and an Osborne caribou was looking me square in the eye, not more than twenty feet away. I shot him in the chest and he ran downhill and fell on the lake shore, less than ten yards from my raft. An Osborne is big and this one was almost as large as a three-year-old moose. Feeling lucky, I dressed and loaded the meat on my raft and headed back up the lake.

A month passed and the weather turned chilly. I set out a trapline for mink and did well. The duck had been gone for some time but there was still plenty of trout, so I didn't lack for food, though I missed having salmon to eat—they had spawned and died. Then, one morning, I stepped out the cabin door and saw something that didn't look too pleasant. The lake had frozen over in a thin sheet of ice.

I went to fish in the river and streams but the trout had gone to the lake when the water got cold and I caught nothing. I believe it was then that I began to have serious thoughts about the coming winter.

The caribou I had shot had weighed well over three hundred pounds. I could have cut much of that into thin strips and smoked it for winter, for my cabin was the perfect smokehouse. A small fire made in a circular hole in the center of the earth floor and fed with dry cottonwood would have given me just the right amount of clean, dry smoke. I could have smoked enough meat and trout and salmon to feed ten men. I had done nothing right.

The lake finally froze over enough for me to walk on it, and I fished through the ice in many places but caught nothing. I didn't know then that in winter the fish go to the deep places in the lake where the water is warmer. I stopped trapping altogether and hunted just for food. The only thing I found was a porcupine once in a while, and then they too were gone. Snow came now, and soon I was in a white, frozen world.

I realized a hard truth at that time. Nature in the summer months is bountiful and generous—birds singing in the trees, ducks in the stream and along the lake shore, busy talking back and forth and looking after their young, fish and game there every day for the taking. Now the only sounds I heard were the loud cracks as ice gave way to pressure, or the wind howling out of the north, bringing more snow. I had wasted the summer and now I knew I was going to be hungry for a long time.

I hunted hard for porcupine now and occasionally I managed to find one that I had missed in early winter. It was barely enough to keep me from starving. The deep snow brought the ptarmigan down from the high slopes but they stayed in the willow growths along the shore and were difficult to get close to. Once in a while I was lucky. Hunger is a good teacher. One day I discovered that when the birds were ready to bed down for the night they would burrow into the snow until they were completely covered. After a while their body heat and breath would form a small round air hole, and if I could get close enough without disturbing them I could put my snowshoe down over the hole, reach in and catch my breakfast. It was slow, cold, wet work, but I got very good at it—and then one morning my food supply wasn't there. I covered many miles on snowshoes and found nothing. I learned much later that ptarmigan feed on willow buds and move on when they have exhausted the supply.

The hard winter brought me some unwanted visitors: I was regularly plagued by shrews, who began to use my cabin as their home. They were so numerous I could sit quietly on the bunk and watch them; sometimes at night while I was asleep they would nibble my neck or hand. Eventually I got tired of the damage they did in the cabin, so I worked on a way to rid myself of their nuisance. I had an empty coffee can and this I buried in the dirt floor so that the top was level with the surface. At night I fastened a small round stick across it but left it loose enough to roll and turn. In the middle of the stick I tied a small piece of porcupine meat. The shrews would run out along the stick but their weight would turn it over, dropping them into the can. There was never more than one live shrew in the can for very long. When the second shrew fell in, it was a fight to the finish and the winner ate the loser and it didn't take long. In the morning there would be a pile of fur, many small bones and one live shrew in the can. I have read since then that a shrew can eat twenty-four hours a day and I believe it. I managed to keep them under control.

❋ ❋ ❋

On the first of March something happened that gave me a choice of two things, and neither of them looked good.

I was carrying a piece of firewood back to the cabin. I had it on my shoulder and somehow I fell, twisting my knee badly. I crawled inside but I knew it would be days before I could walk, still less hunt. I was fortunate in one respect—I had just found what I'll swear was the last porcupine in the entire valley. I rationed myself to one small piece of meat a day, but when I was able to stand on my leg again the only thing in my cabin, in the way of food, was plenty of tea.

Prolonged hunger is an insidious thing. Against your will, it assumes control of your mind. Every thought is of something to eat. Ever-present, gnawing hunger governs every judgment.

I thought about staying where I was, trying to hold out until spring. The ice would be gone then and I could raft all the way to the coast. But I wasn't sure I could last that long. I had to leave for the coast now, while I had enough stamina left to make it. I worried what to take with me, what to leave behind. The furs I had taken had no weight to worry about, but my rifle, the Krag, was heavy and the thought of it hanging from my shoulder decided me: it would have to stay. In any case, there had been no game and I was sure I would find none on the journey. My tarpaulin was heavy, too, and I left that.

It was midnight in the middle of March when I was ready to leave. The moon was full and bright. I stood for a time outside the closed cabin door. There was warmth and shelter there and I hated to leave it, but hunger was there too. I had my furs and my one blanket. I had tea and matches, a camp axe and a small coil of rope.

The silence was so intense it seemed an invisible threat. The mountain ranges to either side were pale shadows. The cold crept through my clothing and told me to move on and I did, the only sound the whisper of my snowshoes as they slid across the soft surface.

After a time, the coming daylight pushed the night away and the mountains were sharp silhouettes against the sky. I reached the end of the lake just as the sun cast a golden promise on the horizon. It was going to be a fine day and what I saw next filled me with joy. The river was wide open. It meant an easy ride on a raft, clear to the coast.

I didn't waste any time. I crossed to a stand of cotton-wood with plenty of dead, dry trees. I cut down and limbed all I would need for a good raft and dragged them to the edge of the river. It didn't seem to matter that my knee ached, for I'd soon be riding the raft. I cut a last long, slender pole to push and steer with, lashed my small pack to the raft securely and pushed away from shore.

The current wasn't very fast but that was because I was still close to the lake. I knew the current would pick up once I moved down the river and got into its turns and bends. After two hours of slow drifting, I went around a sharp turn and my raft came to rest against solid ice. I knew at once the river would be impassable clear to the coast.

The knowledge came to me like a physical blow. I pushed the raft to shore and tossed my pack on the bank. I was angry at the river and I was worn out. I took my pole and pushed the raft as far out in the water as I could and threw the pole after it. I made a fire and rested while I boiled some water. Sipping hot tea took some of the ache out of my bones. It was still early in the day and I decided to set out again. Whenever I came to a ravine with willows growing in it, I stopped and picked a handful of buds. They were dry and hard but they were something to put in my stomach. Every night my bed was the same, a trench scooped out in the snow, some branches laid in the bottom to keep me dry, and a little snow caved in from the sides to cover my blanket. I was warm enough. I lost track of the days, but I believe it was on the fifth day that I went down into a fairly steep ravine. The sun had melted the snow from the bottom and it looked warm down there. A stream trickled along between sandy stretches. I took my snowshoes off and it felt good to walk on bare ground.

There were small footprints in the sand ahead of me. For a few seconds they meant nothing to me and then I realized, with a shock, that I wasn't alone. I knelt down and traced the marks with my fingers. They were so fresh that sand was falling into them from the sides. They went up the steep slope of snow and I crawled after them. As my head reached the top of the slope, I saw four pairs of *mukluk*-clad legs not more than inches from my face.

I looked up and saw the little girl who had made the footprints. Beside her was a young man and a young woman, and an older woman, all of them dressed in fur parkas.

The man reached down, put his hands under my shoulders and helped me to my feet.

"You come slow to this place."

"I travel slow. My knee is bad."

He took my pack and snowshoes.

"You come and you eat." He didn't waste any words. He spoke briefly in Eskimo to the older woman and turned back to me.

"My mother, you go with her."

She smiled and took me by my arm and led me to the tunnel entrance of a small sod hut. There was another hut further off. The entrance to an Eskimo hut always faces south, a rounded tunnel about four feet high and six feet long. An abrupt right turn and another tunnel of the same size and shape brings you to the door. They are made this way to cut the driving force of the wind. It was the first time I had ever been inside a native hut. It was lit by a small seal-gut skylight, the floor was hard-packed dirt and the sod walls had been pounded smooth. There was a wood-burning cook-stove, a small hand-hewn table and a large block of hard-looking wood. A wide pole bunk covered with hay and laced-down reindeer skins had been built against one wall. Everything except the stove was hand-made.

I must have looked tired for the mother took me to the bed and sat me down. She knelt and unlaced my boots and pulled them off and then she pulled my parka off. Smiling, she said something to me and left. She came back soon, carrying a slab of frozen reindeer meat. Putting it on the block and using a hatchet, she chopped off small pieces and tossed them in a pot of boiling water on the stove. It wasn't long before she poured all of it, meat and juice, into a big bowl and gave me a spoon. It was the best food I ever tasted. She took the empty bowl and motioned me to lie down. I was asleep before I had time to think how lucky this day had been.

When I woke it was dark. Someone had covered me with a soft, tanned reindeer skin. I slept again. Next time I woke it was daylight and the mother was there. She smiled and spoke to me and I knew she was saying good morning. I watched as she mixed flour and water in a bowl and cooked pancakes in a skillet. After I had eaten, I asked her about Togiak. I knew the word Togiak would let her know what I meant. She went outside and soon her son came in. He sat down on the bed by me.

"When you come, you look bad. You stay one more day. You eat and sleep."

"Tell me, how far is Togiak?"

"For you, maybe five, six days. You go slow. Where did you come from?"

"Togiak Lake."

"You hunt fur?"

"Yes, I trapped. Tell me, you live here where the wind is strong—no trees, just open tundra. Down in the river bottom you could have trees, you could make log houses."

He nodded. "Yes, it is bad here now. One time, maybe my father's father's time, there was plenty caribou. They could see them far off. They see them come and they wait. When the snow is gone, I think maybe we go to the coast. Some of my people there. We live there, hunt the seal and the walrus." He got to his feet. "One more day, maybe you feel good."

He left me then. I thought of the caribou migration trail that came down into Togiak Valley through the pass I had been in. He was right. Once this had been a good place but not now, not ever again for them. Guiltily, I realized I had said nothing about gold, but perhaps it wouldn't have interested him. I slept off and on during the day, and his mother fed me. I have been in many Eskimo huts since then but I don't believe I have ever seen people who had less than that family. Whatever they had they shared with me and I thought again of the signs I had seen in the restaurant windows in Anchorage a year ago.

I slept well that night and in the morning felt ready to travel again. I didn't look forward to the trip but I was anxious to reach the coast. I tied the thongs of my snowshoes round my ankles and slipped the straps of my pack over my shoulders. The son came to me with a piece of reindeer meat and dropped it into my pack. "This will be good tonight."

I left them and after a bit I looked back. They were still watching me and they waved. I raised my hand in the air and kept on going. I never even learned their names.

✳ ✳ ✳

When the daylight began to fade I made camp, boiled the meat in the tea can and ate it. My eyes were smarting and felt irritated, and I knew they were suffering from the bright sun on the snow and the acrid smoke from my alder wood fire. The next day was sunny and bright again and I made a good distance, but my eyes were giving me quite a bit of trouble. They felt as though sand had been thrown in them. That evening I came upon a herd of at least two thousand reindeer, the main Togiak herd, as I learned later. I wished then that I had not left my rifle back at the cabin. I made a cold camp that night. There was no brush anywhere for shelter or heat and as far as I could see, there was no ravine. I scooped out a trench in the snow long enough for me, pulled my blanket round me and laid down, dropping the parka hood over my face. The wind had picked up and I caved the sides of the trench in, enough to give me a good cover. I packed the snow, pushing it away from my face and pulled back the parka hood. I had a clear space for my face, I was secure and I was warm. Some time that night, I woke up to the sound of wolves howling. I knew they were after the reindeer. Before very long, everything was quiet again. At daybreak I could see three patches of bloody snow. The wolves had taken what they needed for food and the reindeer had moved up the valley. I hoped the friends I had left would see them.

It was then that a thought came to mind: the wolves would probably have left something. I went to each of the kills and found four nice long leg bones. They had been cleaned of meat but what I wanted was inside. I put the bones in my pack and started on again. It was another day of bright sun and by mid-afternoon I was almost snow-blind. If I had known to rub charcoal under my eyes it would have prevented that, but there were many things then that I didn't know. Towards evening, I stopped at the first wooded ravine I came to. I built a big fire, for I wanted a good bed of coals. After the fire burned down I took the bones the wolves had left me and laid them side by side on the glowing coals and waited anxiously. It took some time and then there was a sharp crack. One of the bones had split its entire length. With a little help from my axe, I soon had it laid wide open, and the rich marrow was there. Bone marrow is good at any time, but for me, then, it was something special. I cleaned out all four and settled down to sleep.

The next morning my eyes were still bad. A night's rest hadn't helped them much. I kept my direction the best way I knew, by holding the sun on my left side; that would keep me heading south. By mid-afternoon, with the sun on my right side now, I came on a sod hut. I went inside and it looked as though no one had been there for a long time. I decided to go no further that day and to spend the night inside. Wondering how much further I would have to travel to reach the coast, I walked out of the hut. The top of it looked warm and dry so I climbed up and sat there for some time. I heard a sound then, a sound I hadn't heard in a long time. Somewhere, dogs were barking, but almost at once the sound stopped.

I rose to my feet and shouted as loud as I could. I heard the sound of sled runners slicing over the snow. The dogs stopped close by and I slid down the side of the hut and walked over. An Eskimo boy was the driver. He smiled.

"I didn't know what you were until you stood up. Your eyes are bad from the sun. Where did you come from?"

"From the lake, at the head of the river. Did you come from the coast?"

"Yes, I live on the coast. My name is Wasilly."

"What are you doing way out here?"

"I'm looking for reindeer. The wolves keep them moving."

"With your dogs, maybe three hours back that way where I came from, there are plenty of reindeer. The wolves are with them now."

"I'll tell my father and we'll come back."

"My name is Fred. Can I ride with you?"

"Of course. You will come home with me."

We put my pack and snowshoes in the sled. I stood on one runner and Wasilly stood on the other; we each had a handle to hang on to. He spoke to his dogs, they tightened the traces and we were off.

3 / *The Bering Sea Coast*

IN LESS THAN TWO HOURS we reached his home, a large sod hut set on a knoll. The Bering Sea, not far away and still frozen solid, was covered with rolling ridges of snow.

Wasilly turned the sled on its side to hold his dogs, and led me inside. I had learned about my new friend on the drive. His father and mother went to Bristol Bay every summer, a hundred and fifty miles east, to work in the salmon canneries. The white man's economy had forced most of the coastal people to do the same or, if they were fortunate, they could fish in one of the wooden sailboats; but salmon canning was the big industry in Bristol Bay. Wasilly had learned to speak English by being around white people there. His father and mother, he said, didn't care to learn.

His parents had heard the dogs approach and were standing when we came in. Wasilly spoke to his mother in Eskimo and she came forward, motioning me to take off my parka. That done, she led me to the table. Almost at once, she brought a large platter, heaped with creamed salmon, which she set in front of me, placing a spoon beside it. I waited for a plate. She spoke to Wasilly.

"My mother says for you to eat."

I ate all of it. It was only early evening but my day had been long and after the meal I was glad when Wasilly told me to lie down and rest. The bed was wide and long, made of the usual poles, hay and reindeer skins. As I sat on the end to take off my boots I saw there was a little boy lying on the bed, covered up and quiet.

"Is this your little brother? Isn't he well?"

"For a long time he has been hurting, here." Wasilly placed a hand on his chest. The little boy turned his head and looked at me and I suppose he wondered who I was and where I had come from, but before I knew it I was sleeping.

It was after daylight next morning when I awoke. The mother was sitting at the table. No one else was there. The little boy was gone and I was glad he was better. I lay still for a while. It was good to be rested and not to have to worry. Wasilly came into the hut.

"Is your brother better?"

He had been a happy boy yesterday, smiling and talking, but not now. He looked at me and shook his head.

"Last night my brother died."

I looked at his mother then. She was staring at her folded hands. I didn't know what to do and there was nothing I could say. All night long I had rested and my bone-weary tiredness was gone. That night too a little boy had lain by my side and his life had slipped away.

"My father says you must go soon. The ice will be leaving the river."

"I'll get ready."

I pulled on my boots and got into my parka. I went to the little boy's mother and put my hand on hers. I could see the grief on her face and she turned away.

Outside the dogs were ready to go, straining at their traces, the father holding the lead dog. I went to him, took his hand and said the empty words, "I'm sorry."

Wasilly was standing on one of the runners and I stood on the other, just as we had the day before. He spoke to the dogs and they made a turn along the side of the hut. I saw the small form there. The body of the little boy had been wrapped in reindeer skins and tied to the roof where it would wait until the snow went away and some of the frost had left the unyielding earth. I was angry at life's grim necessity. After a while I stole a glance at Wasilly. He was staring straight ahead, stoically. He was twelve years old.

After an hour we crossed the mouth of the Togiak river. Wasilly's father had been right. Trickles of water were running over the surface of the ice. The river would go out before long.

"Where are we going?"

"There's a trader who lives down the coast. It isn't far. You will be better there." Wasilly looked down at my ragged pants. "You need some clothes."

Ahead of us I could see a small white frame house standing back from the beach; in five minutes we were there. Wasilly stopped his dogs in front of the house and I took my pack and snowshoes from the sled.

"Are you going to Bristol Bay and Dillingham this summer?"

"Yes, we will be there."

"I'll look for you."

We shook hands and he turned his dogs and headed back the way we had come. I stared after him. A little boy, I thought, and a man so soon, too soon. I heard a door open and close.

"I'm Chris Peterson."

I turned and saw a rawboned, lined face with a smile on it.

"I'm Fred Hatfield. Wasilly lost his brother last night."

Chris cupped his hands to his mouth. "Wasilly!" he shouted. The dogs came to a stop and Wasilly looked back.

With his arm Chris motioned for him to return and the dogs swung around.

"Let's go in, Fred."

When I stepped inside I entered a new world. Martha Peterson was a very pretty woman and wore a neat dress. There were soft easy chairs and a couch. The wall on the far side of the room was lined with bookshelves from ceiling to floor, and they were filled.

"Fred, sit down and wait for us. We've got to get some things together for Wasilly's mother." They carried out boxes, filled mostly with food. I heard the sled move off and the Petersons came back indoors, their faces saddened. For a moment I was back in Wasilly's house, seeing the quiet, grieving face of his mother.

"Chris, what was wrong with the little boy?"

"Tuberculosis. It takes a lot of our people."

Martha looked me over as I stood up and pulled off my parka. I unlaced my boots and got them off. My socks were strips of burlap from flour sacks, wrapped round my feet and lower legs.

"Fred, by the looks of your clothes, you've been somewhere for a long time."

"I lived for a year at the head of Togiak Lake."

She brought a tray and placed it on my lap. It had been a while since I had seen bacon and eggs and fresh crisp toast.

"Your eyes are in bad shape, too, but I can take care of them. Eat your breakfast and then we'll get busy."

Chris rocked in his chair for a while. "Whatever made you go into Togiak Lake? It isn't really a good fur country."

I told him about the large gold nugget that had made news in the Anchorage paper.

"Fred, somewhere around Togiak Lake there's gold. There was a white man who came here looking for gold and two of our people took him up the Togiak River. After some time he came back and he had a lot of gold but he was alone.

My people asked him where the two men were. He said they had died. My people killed him and threw away his gold. They knew he lied."

"Where did they throw it?"

"If I knew that, Fred, I'd have it. I was a young boy then, but I remember and I know it happened.

"I think I'm about sixty years old. I was born on the Togiak River, I'm not sure just where. Martha and I are both part-Eskimo. My father and mother and my brothers and sisters were all taken by smallpox. I was one of the lucky ones. I lived through it. When I was about ten years old, the people I was living with took me with them to Bristol Bay. There were fur traders there then and a few white trappers. I learned English by listening to them talk, then I started buying books and magazines, anything I could find. I taught myself to read and write. I taught Martha. You stayed with two families on your way out from the lake—how many of the people could speak English?"

"There was a young man with the first family, and then there was Wasilly. He speaks real well."

"Most of them don't want to learn. They remember the stories that tell them the way things used to be. They won't accept the truth, that the old ways can never come back. We both read a lot, Martha and me. Whatever we know comes from those books."

Martha came back into the room.

"Chris, bring in the big tub and put it in the corner over there. I've got water on the stove."

She laid some clothes over a chair. "Fred, these fit Chris, so they'll be a little big for you but they'll do well enough."

Chris brought in the tub and filled it with warm water, Martha brought towels and soap and they left me alone. I don't think anything had ever felt as good as that warm water. I washed and scrubbed and finally got into my new clothes. I called for Chris and he took my old ones away just as Martha returned, with a basin in her hands.

"Fred, you'll have to lie down on the couch. I've got warm water and soda here and I'm going to lay a cloth over your eyes. I'll change it pretty often, so it will stay moist."

By the third day my eyes were fine. For two days the world had come to me through my ears and in those two days I learned a lot. Chris was a living history of Alaska and its people. He knew that the coast of the Bering Strait was fifty-five miles from Siberia, that the coastline of Alaska was greater in length than that of the United States. Vitus Bering had sighted Alaska in 1741, sighted it and claimed it for Russia. The fact that there were thousands of native people living there at that time, people who thought the land was theirs, made no difference; it belonged to Russia. Gregory Shellikov founded the first colony at Kodiak in 1784. There were hundreds of people living in many villages on Kodiak at that time, but that made no difference either. In 1867 the United States purchased Alaska from Russia for $7.2 million. They were buying stolen property, but that made no difference.

During their occupation, the Russians had moved up the Yukon River, building large log warehouses to store furs. If the Eskimos on the river didn't want to exchange their fur for useless trade tokens, they were driven from the river. The river to the Eskimos was their life: without the salmon to smoke and dry for winter they couldn't survive. So they had to give in to the Russians. The Russians took the furs and they took the prettiest of the young women, too. Any man or boy who protested was shot. At Kodiak the Aleut people were no more than slaves, forced to hunt fur seal and otter for the Russians, and to provide women. In return, the Russians brought them gifts of smallpox, syphilis and tuberculosis.

All these things Chris told me. He said that when the snow left that spring he would show me what smallpox had done to the once large village of Togiak: for three miles at the back of his house there were a hundred small mounds, mounds that at one time had been sod homes.

On the third day he showed me a long slope above his house and told me there were countless graves there. All had died from smallpox. There were no able-bodied people to dig graves, so shallow trenches, inches deep, were scooped out and the bodies placed in and covered with moss. All around, he said, the ground was scattered with the bones of those who had died there, the living too weak to care for them. It wasn't a pretty story.

"Fred, my people live with death riding on their shoulder. If they get sick, they either get well or they die. They know it and they are used to it. Perhaps, someday, things will change."

❊ ❊ ❊

It was April now. The snow and ice had melted from the sea shore and far out on the Bering Sea there were patches of open water.

Chris was a trader. A small galvanized tin warehouse held a supply of flour and sugar and every fall he smoked hundreds of pounds of salmon. There was always plenty hanging there. The Eskimos brought their fur to him to exchange for whatever supplies they needed. Sometimes they didn't have fur, but they were given what they had to have anyway.

People began to arrive from somewhere. One of them brought a side of reindeer, another came with a gift of walrus meat. A little darker than beef, walrus has much the same grain texture and taste. Martha took some, cut it in small squares and boiled it until it was tender. Each of us had a small bowl of fresh, golden-colored seal oil, and with our forks we dipped in pieces of meat. The oil was delicious, with a very mild, nutty flavor, and plenty of fresh-baked bread to go with it. I had spent my winter going hungry. Now, every meal Martha fixed was something to look forward to. One day Chris asked me if I liked raw fish: knowing the way Martha cooked, I was willing to take a risk if she chose to serve up something raw. One visitor had brought in some whitefish. Chris boned it and turned it over to Martha who cut it in wafer-thin slices. It was icy cold and very, very good.

"Fred, you've had walrus meat and you've eaten raw fish and I know you've heard how Eskimos bury fish in the ground and eat it after it's rotten. Let me tell you, the only places where they bury fish in the ground is where they have permafrost. They call it *tipmuk*; perhaps that's their word for keeping, or frozen. They cut a deep hole in the permafrost, put their fish in it and after it's covered over it will keep for a long time. When they take it out to use it will be frozen almost solid. They eat whale blubber, too, not because they have any special liking for it, though. They eat it because it is food and one thing they won't do is waste food. They've had too many hungry times."

I walked out later on the flat behind the house and found the small mounds Chris had told me about; the sad bones were everywhere. I found two complete skeletons side by side. It seemed strange that nothing had been disturbed but it was so. I stooped to feel with the palm of my hand the ground along the sides of the bones, and along the narrow space between them. There I found a small round tunnel, in the grass roots, and followed it with my fingers. At its end was an ivory spear head; the shaft had rotted away long ago, but the spear head was a beautiful piece of workmanship. I wondered why the two bodies were lying side by side. Perhaps a man and his wife. Perhaps, but who knows?

Martha had a brother and one day he showed up. His name was Evan and he was eighteen. We got along fine and hunted geese together and took care of the herring net that was set out from the beach. One day he told me that up on the slope were the graves where an old chief had been buried, with a can of gold buried beside him.

"How do you know a thing like that?"

"I know because they have said so. There is a small dog sled on his grave, a sled with ivory runners."

I gave that some thought and found that I still had a small touch of gold fever.

"Would anyone care if we looked?" I thought of Martha. She still held to the old beliefs.

"There is no one, unless perhaps the Great Spirit. Tell me, Fred, you believe in this one they call God?"

Evan had a sense of humor and I looked at him suspiciously. His eyes and face were serious.

"Evan, there is no difference between the Great Spirit and God. It is all the same."

"No, it is not the same. When the white men talk with their God they must go into a house, a church house. When we talk with our Great Spirit we must be where we can see the sky and the mountains. Even if many of us gather at one time, we must be where we can see these things."

"Evan, it *is* like I said. There is no difference. I feel as your people do. I feel much closer to the Great Spirit, or God, when I am outside and see all of these things. I don't go to a church house to talk to God. I know many of my people do— perhaps it's so they can be close together, out of the wind and rain. But as long as we believe in something good, it is enough."

"Fred, you and me are friends. If you want to look, you go. I will go back to the house."

"Evan, this is a small thing. The Great Spirit wouldn't mind. We need rifles and we need boots. Look at my clothes. They belong to Chris. We could buy all these things and there would still be gold left."

I found I was talking to his back, for he had turned away, back to the house.

I went on up the slope. The graves were easy to find. Each one was a small depression. Using both hands, I grasped the moss and pulled it back: there were men, women and children. Each of them had been placed there with their own treasures. The men had their spear heads, the women their bone or ivory sewing awls and the children their bone or ivory playthings.

Finally I felt something hard, buried in the moss. I pulled it up and it was what I had been looking for—a piece of ivory, four feet long. The sled runner had been in two pieces, joined together with ivory pins. Now I felt close to victory. I grasped the moss and tore it out.

On the chief's chest was a can, solid rust but large enough to hold plenty of gold. I leaned forward and took it from him. It was heavy and I was rich. I broke it open on my knee and it was filled with pieces of quartz, all different colors.

I had a thought that perhaps the Great Spirit, just to teach a greedy man a lesson, had changed gold into quartz. I squeezed the can back together and put it back where it belonged. I covered the grave then and walked down the hill. Evan didn't ask me what I had found and I didn't tell him.

❄ ❄ ❄

Chris had a boat that he used to transport supplies from Bristol Bay. Forty feet long, it had been set up on tressels for the winter and needed a lot of work. Grateful for a chance to repay their kindness, I scraped the old paint off, cleaned out the seams and recaulked them. It was an old boat and the keel seemed soft and spongy, but I did the best I could and finally gave it a paint job. On the bow, I traced the words "The Togiak Queen."

With the waters clearing, we launched the boat for a trial run. Chris had done a lot of work on the motor and we moved along to a reassuring thump.

On the first of June Chris and I stored some supplies on board and were ready to depart; two men and their wives were journeying to Dillingham with us. Our boat wasn't too fast, but the weather was good and all morning we made decent time. That afternoon, though, the seas picked up under a southwesterly wind. Cape Protection was in sight in the distance, but trying to round its point in heavy seas and a small boat appealed to none of us. We pulled in to shore and anchored in the next bay, protected from the wind. That night, one of the women who was with us gave birth to her baby.

When we left the next morning the weather was fair but soon enough it changed again and whitecaps washed over the bow. I thought of the spongy keel beneath us. I think Chris did too.

"Fred, should we turn back?" He had to shout so I could hear him over the sound of the gale force wind.

"How far to Cape Protection?"

"About an hour. It's the same if we turn back, at least an hour to shelter."

There was only one choice. As we neared Cape Protection the shoreline changed to high cliff, straight up and down; the breakers, smashing against its base, made a jagged white line. We made it round the point and suddenly we were in good water again.

We arrived in Dillingham late that afternoon and tied up at the trading company dock. Chris had people to see so I picked up my pack and told him I'd be down in the morning to see him off. I walked up to the trading store and went in. A year ago I had walked through this same door. The same man was there who had sold me supplies then.

"I've got some fur to get rid of."

He nodded.

"You were in here last spring, you've been gone a while. Our fur room is in the back."

I followed him and arranged my furs on a wide counter. He looked them over and made me an offer.

"I'm paying you top price for your fur. It's prime and well cared for. Come back in the store. I'd like to talk to you."

A small corner of the store was railed off. That was his office.

"I'm Howard Griffin and everyone calls me Tubby. Before long, boats will be coming down the rivers. They'll be coming every day. I'm going to need some help. Can you grade fur?"

"Yes, I know fur pretty well."

"If you think you'd like to give me a hand here, I'll give you a list quoting our prices. We run a small liquor store in the evenings. That would be your job, too. I'll pay you five dollars a day, a nice cabin to live in and all you can eat in our restaurant."

I think it was the "all you can eat" that made up my mind and we shook hands to close the deal. He showed me where I could find what I wanted for clothing and went outside with me and showed me where I was going to live.

The next morning I went down to the dock to see Chris but no one was there and the boat was gone. Our boat had brought us safely into port, but her old keel had finally given way, and she was resting on the bottom, in ten feet of water.

❆ ❆ ❆

In the spring of 1935 Dillingham was a rough town, a gathering place for all the trappers who worked the big rivers, the Nushagak and the Mulchatna. On the first of May the boats started to arrive from upriver and every day brought more. The little village took on a lively pace. There were a lot of good men there, and there were some not so good.

The liquor store I ran in the evenings was always busy. For some of the men, and some of the women too, drinking seemed to be their main form of recreation. I was so new in town I didn't know any of my customers. One man told me his name was Cannibal John. When I asked him why he had a name like that, he said he had bitten a man's nose off one time and that was the name they gave him. I know he did, because that summer I saw the man he'd worked on; where his nose had been were two round holes.

One night the movies were just over—the theater was close by and business always picked up at that time—and four or five women came in and sat down on cases of beer stacked against the wall. The door opened and a man came in. I'd never seen him before.

"Marguerite, you ready to go?"

"No, I've got a date with Fred here."

He stared. "A date with that punk? All right then."

I took a good look at him. He was big enough, but he was a little puffy where he shouldn't have been.

"What did you call me?"

"You heard. If you don't like it, step outside."

"I'll be right with you."

He stepped outside and I took off my jacket. It was a Pendleton and it had cost me five dollars, a day's wages.

"What's wrong with that guy?"

"Everything. He's just no good."

"Who is he?"

"His name is Dixie Whittington."

"You girls are going to have to leave. I'll be outside for a little while."

I folded my jacket, laid it on the counter and went outside and locked the door.

I saw Dixie and what seemed like all the people in town gathered around him in a semicircle.

I knew exactly how I was going to handle him. I had every intention of driving my foot into his belly before he had time to grunt. As I walked toward him, I found my hunting knife had worked its way round to the front, so I slid it back to the side, where it would be out of the way. When I put my pants on in the morning, my knife went on with them. It was always on my belt and had been for over a year now.

When I stopped walking I was about six feet from Dixie. My knife had a ten-inch blade and it was heavy enough to cut down a small sapling; when it was in its sheath, it looked a lot longer. I watched Dixie and I saw his eyes follow my hand. He seemed fascinated by the knife and I could see no reason to take my hand from it.

"They tell me your name is Dixie. What did you call me?"

"I didn't call you nothing."

"Yes, you did. You called me a punk and you might just as well have spit in my face. You had no reason."

"Let me buy you a drink."

"No, I buy my own whisky. Dixie, I'm going to tell you something. If you ever bother me again, in any way, I'll open your guts up clear to your chin. If I were you, I think I'd leave town. Just go somewhere else. All these people here know you and some of them are going to see you every day. They'll know what you are. Just a big man with a big mouth."

I turned and left him then and went back into the shop. It was getting chilly and I put my jacket back on. I was relieved, for I had expected some kind of a time outside. I know it isn't good to demean a man the way I had him, but he had brought it on himself. I'd like to say that I wouldn't use a knife on any man, unless it was a case of life or death. It wasn't long before I found out all about Dixie. He had a bad habit of pushing the native boys around. Anyone smaller than Dixie was fair game, if he was sure of them. He had a cabin and a complete outfit up on the Mulchatna River but I heard he left it all behind. That summer he fished for a cannery over around Naknek, but he never came back to Dillingham.

❄   ❄   ❄

Myron Moran had his own plane. He came to see me one day.

"Fred, did you ever get into that high pass that heads west from the Upper Togiak Lake?"

I told him I had spent some time there.

"Did you find any sign of an old cabin?" I said that I had.

"Well now, a few years ago an old man came into Dillingham with all the gold he could pack on his back. He had a cabin in that pass. What do you say? If you'll go back there with me, I'll pay all expenses."

I remembered some hard times in Togiak. I hadn't told anyone about my find at the second creek or my plans to go back there and I wasn't sure I wanted to.

"Maybe sometime, Myron. Not right away."

Matt Flenzburg stopped in to see me.

"Fred, did you go panning around that old cabin?"

I told him I hadn't.

"You should have. A lot of gold came from that creek."

I had been in town about a month. One day, leaning in the doorway, I watched an Eskimo woman coming up the boardwalk from the dock. She was dressed in a heavy cotton replica of the winter parka that was made of furs; the cloth hood had ruffled edges sewn on it. It was Wasilly's mother. I went inside to the candy shelf and got down the biggest box of chocolates there; it was tied with ribbons and bows. She came into the store and sat down without speaking on the long wooden bench against the wall, waiting. I walked over and placed the box in her lap. She looked up. I had seen her only one day and the next sad morning. For the first time I saw her smile. She was beautiful. I bent down and hugged her.

They had come for the summer work. Bristol Bay had the largest salmon run of any place in the world—it still has. There were several canneries and a small town at the mouth of every river that emptied into the bay, the Nushagak, the Ugashik, the Egigik and the Naknek. Most of the fishermen and the cannery crews were shipped up from the States, but there were numbers of native people employed as well. On the first of June the canneries started to get ready: the fishing season started on June 25 and ended on July 25. For that month the little river towns became rough places. The men from outside considered the native people trash and the resident white people weren't thought of as much better. At night some of the outside men roamed through our village. Any men with families kept their wives and daughters at home. It wasn't a good situation. It was a matter of protecting your own people and it didn't take me long to learn the way things were. Most of my friends were native people, and they surely had my respect and support.

4 / *Klutuk*

Breakup was a big event in the spring. It meant that all of the men who worked the big rivers for fur would arrive after a long spell in isolation. They seemed almost to follow the last of the ice as it swept the rivers clear and floated out to sea.

I got to know quite a few of them. They were all older than I was, and some of them had strange names: "Butch Smith" . . . "Kid Wilkins" . . . "Wood River Chris" . . . "Big John" . . . "Happy Jack Smith." I never knew what their real names were—I don't think anyone did—but I used to wonder what kind of a past they had had. There was "Deep Hole Tom"; his name was easy to understand. It seems that "Deep Hole" would dig a vertical shaft, ninety feet down at times, if he thought there was a prehistoric stream bed beneath. He would do this simply because he had known a man once who had done that very thing and had found an old stream bed that was almost half gold in places.

I met the Platinum King. He was an Eskimo boy from Nome, not more than twenty-five years old. This side of Nome he had prospected a creek and found a greyish looking metal, with a trace of gold. He sold his claims to a mining syndicate for a winter's grubstake and when I asked him he said they had told him the grey metal wasn't worth much.

The town of Platinum was born right there and millions were taken from his claims. It seems that if some people get the chance to drive the shaft into you, they drive it in deep. I believe that's called good business.

After I got to know them well, I found these men were all the kind who would go that long extra mile for a friend. I knew Butch Smith especially well. He must have been close to seventy years old but he was in fine shape. He had wide shoulders, his face was lined and his eyes were like two pieces of blue glacier ice. One day he asked me if I planned to trap in the coming winter and I told him I was looking for a good place.

"The big rivers are too crowded, Fred. You're young and I have a place in mind would suit you."

He told me about the Tikchik Lakes. It was fine fur country, with plenty of game.

"There used to be a man named Harry Stevens who trapped that country. I spent one fall in there with Harry—I was prospecting. Two years ago a plane flew in to pick him up and he wasn't where he'd said he'd meet the plane. So the pilot came out and picked me up and we covered every one of Harry's cabins. I knew them all. He hadn't been in any of them for some time.

"He's in there somewhere, Fred. It's just that one day Harry didn't make it back to his cabin. It's grizzly country and that might have been it, and the river ice can be bad when it's covered with snow. 'Most anything can happen to a man and if he's too far from home he doesn't make it. I've got a cabin in town, Fred—you've never been there. If you want to, we'll go to my place and I'll fix a map for you. I'll mark all of the places where Harry's cabins are. They'll still be in good shape."

It wasn't far to his cabin; it wasn't far to anywhere in Dillingham. Inside was an Eskimo woman and like Butch, she was along in years.

"Fred, this is my wife, Mary. Take a chair by the table and we'll have coffee." Butch brought a map to the table and sat down by me.

"These are the Tikchiks, five big lakes tied together by rivers. These are Harry's cabins. I'll mark them for you."

There was Cow Pond and Rat Lake. There was a cabin at the mouth of Rat Creek where it entered the Tikchik river. At the head of the Nuyakuk river, at the foot of the first lake, was another cabin. It looked like a wonderful country and a good chance for me. We talked a while and finally Butch turned to me.

"Fred, there's something I've got to tell you and then you can make up your mind about that country. Last year the bodies of three government surveyors were taken from the Nushagak river, at Ekwok. All three of them had been shot. Opinion seemed to be that the job had been done by an Eskimo who lived a long ways up the Nushagak, name of Klutuk. Well, he lived at the mouth of Klutuk Creek and that's what people called him. He never came down the river in the spring like everyone else. He hated white men.

"Me and Kid Wilkins and Sam Donaldson agreed to go up the river and bring him into town for questioning. I knew Klutuk better than any other white man and I thought I could bring him in with no trouble. It took us ten days to get to his place and he seemed willing enough to come downriver with us.

"We made camp the first night and Kid and me, we left Sam to watch Klutuk while we went to see if we could find some meat. When we came back, Klutuk wasn't there but Sam was. He was lying by the campfire with our double-bitted axe driven into his head. I had known Sam a good many years and he wasn't a careless man, but he was careless that night. He let Klutuk get behind him.

"We buried Sam and came back down the river. No one ever went looking for Klutuk again. They wouldn't know where to start looking. I know a lot of the native boys up there. I know Klutuk traps and he brings the fur to his people. They furnish him with supplies and news." Butch got up and came back with more coffee.

"What has this got to do with the Tikchiks?"

"All I can do is tell you what I think, Fred, but I believe I'm right. The King Salmon River isn't very far from Klutuk's place and the headwaters of that river drain down from the northeast plateau of the Tikchiks. It's good caribou country and I think Klutuk has his camp there. I suppose you'll winter this year at the foot of the first lake. That would put you about forty miles from Klutuk. That's quite far, so you shouldn't have to worry about him. On the other hand, Klutuk is a smart old man. If I were you, I'd keep my eyes open.

"You're young and I have an idea you're pretty handy. You'll be all right. But I want you to do a favor for me. An old friend of mine, Jake Savolly, has a cabin about fifteen miles down the Nuyakuk—he travels by boat and there's a bad set of falls there, so that's as far as he goes. Jake doesn't do much trapping, he just winters there more than anything. Well, he didn't show up this spring. He always has plenty of supplies at his cabin and he could hold out for a long time. But he might have had an accident. 'Most any little thing could keep him from being able to handle his boat for the trip downriver. I wish you'd check on him. It would be about a day's hike for you. His cabin is on the west side of the river."

I told Butch of course I would and I got ready to leave. He gave me the map he had marked.

"You'll be flying in with Matt Flenzburg. He knows all these locations. If I don't see you again here, have a good winter and I'll see you in the spring."

It was too late in the year for me to try for a fishing job with anyone and I worked for Tubby Griffin all summer. On the first of August I talked to Matt Flenzburg, who said he could fly me in to the Tikchiks any time. We left a few days later. His plane was on floats and he landed me at the foot of the first lake, not more than five minutes' walk from Harry Stevens' cabin at the head of the Nuyakuk. We unloaded my supplies. This time I had plenty of everything; I didn't want another Togiak winter. I told Matt to pick me up the middle of April while there would still be good solid ice on the lake for his plane skis. He left and I carried my first load of supplies down to the cabin. It was a nice place and it was easy to see that Harry had taken a lot of care when he built it: a good big window on either side and plenty of room for everything. I got settled down and on the third day I was ready to do as Butch had asked me. Early in the morning I set out for Jake Savolly's cabin. Fifteen miles wasn't too far but I passed several places where grizzlies had hauled salmon from the river, so I didn't travel fast and kept an eye out for them. Bears are touchy when they're feeding. It took me about five hours to reach Jake's cabin.

It was built on a high bank overlooking the river. The falls Butch had told me about were there and I could understand why Jake hadn't come any further. As I got nearer, somehow the cabin didn't look as though it had been used for some time. The door was only fastened with a latch. I raised it up and went in. The only things there were the stove with the stove pipe still in place and a small pile of wood stacked against the wall and a chair. Every trapper saves empty coffee cans—they have a dozen uses—but here there was nothing. It seemed odd. I was a little tired. I always carried my tea can with me. It had been a three-pound lard pail; it had a bail and a tight-fitting cover and I kept a small cloth bag of tea in it. Hot tea is fine for tired bones. I started a fire in the stove and went down to the river for water. There was Jake's boat, pulled back from the river far enough so that the winter ice couldn't reach it. He must have done that in the previous fall. I was puzzled now. Jake clearly hadn't used his cabin or his boat for a long time. I got my water and went back to the cabin. After I set the can on to heat I took the hand-made chair and pulled it over by the stove. I don't know whether it was the dozens of small squeakings or the nibbles on my hand and wrist that roused me—my pants were a moving blanket of shrews. I jumped up and stamped and brushed them off and they disappeared into their crevices and holes. I didn't know there could be that many shrews in one place but they were there.

I had planned to spend the night in the cabin but not now. I drank my tea and went outside, staring down toward Jake's boat. I walked toward the back of the cabin and there he was. He had been dragged there, for his arms were stretched above his head, and he'd been lying there for a long time. There wasn't much left, just bones, and the shrews had polished those clean. Bones and a few shreds of cloth. I looked him over carefully. One of his ribs had been cut by a bullet, about four inches from the spine.

I stood there for a while. I found that I was angry and there was a cold feeling in me. I knew Klutuk had been there.

This was something that Klutuk hadn't had to do. Jake could never have known who he was or why or even if he was in the country. Klutuk may have thought he had some kind of an excuse for his other killings, but not for this one.

I went back to the front of the cabin and sat down in the open doorway to work things out. On the water sound carries for a long way. Klutuk had heard Jake's outboard motor above the falls and after the first good snowfall he had moved in. Klutuk used a dog team, that I already knew from Butch. In winter, native men travel with a dog team; in the summer months, it was strictly by canoe. He had tied his dogs maybe three miles from the cabin so they couldn't be heard and he'd walked in. Jake had been easy to kill. Klutuk had brought his dogs to the cabin and loaded Jake's supplies. The outboard motor was gone, too. It must have meant at least two trips for Klutuk back to his place.

I had enough daylight left to make it back to my own cabin and I started off. My mind was busy with thoughts of Klutuk and a way to get to him, for I surely meant to have him. A raging bellow brought me back to reality and the wide-open mouth and big form of a grizzly, clawing up the short steep bank. I didn't aim. I didn't have to. When my finger touched the trigger the muzzle of my rifle was no more than two feet from his jaws. He slid back and came to a stop by the water's edge. I could see the white bones of his skull. My bullet had entered his mouth and taken the back of his head off.

I tried to keep Klutuk out of my mind now and pay attention to the trail ahead of me. I couldn't forget that Jake had been man number five for Klutuk. I didn't intend to be number six.

It was almost black-dark when I got home. Inside I fastened blankets over the windows before I lit the lamp. It's odd in a way, how quickly a cabin becomes home. I had been here only three days and this cabin was new to me; even so, it was home. When I think about it, that was the first place I had ever had that I could call mine.

I spent the next two or three days giving a lot of thought about how to handle Klutuk. I knew he must have heard the drone of the plane and seen it set down at the foot of the lake. From his point of view there wouldn't be any great need for care. He would know where I was and that I was just a visitor. After the first good snow he could move in, chain up his dogs and in a short time he could have me lined up in his rifle sights. He might guess that I knew who he was and where he was but he couldn't be sure. I intended to change that situation. I wanted Klutuk to feel that I was hunting him. I wanted to make him very careful. That was all I wanted for this winter. I knew he wouldn't give up, that he'd still try for me, but he'd have to change his plans and I had every intention of making his plans for him.

I stayed pretty well under cover. I didn't do any trapping. That would puzzle him and I wanted him puzzled. I wanted him worried. I thought I knew the way his mind worked. I didn't think a man like him would travel overland much in my direction but I couldn't be sure. I waited for snow, for snow would play a big part in my plans for Klutuk.

When the weather got cold enough, I shot a moose for my winter's meat. I cut the hide in two pieces and used them to cover my windows at night—the blankets I had been using I needed now, for the nights were chilly.

Finally the snow came. It came down steadily and in no time at all there was a good foot of it, fine for snowshoes. I made up a pack and set out, heading due north. Butch had told me he thought Klutuk would have his camp at the head of the King Salmon and I believed him. I didn't travel fast. I listened for the bark of a dog, anything that would tell me about Klutuk. The days were still fairly long and even at the pace I traveled, I believe I covered twenty miles. I made a cold camp that night. The smoke from a fire would have alerted dogs if Klutuk was in the area and I didn't want him to know he had a visitor. Not yet. After five miles next morning I found what I was looking for: a dog-team trail, following the side of a still-open stream. I stayed on it and came to Klutuk's first mink set. I pulled his trap and snapped it shut, placing it carefully on the bank of the stream where it could be seen. I found perhaps twenty sets and pulled them all. I headed home then. I circled round and cut back on my trail many times. Though the marks of my snowshoes could be seen, Klutuk wouldn't follow that kind of trail very far: he'd never know where I might be waiting for him.

I made another cold camp that night but I was satisfied now. Klutuk would have to quit trapping—he'd never know where I might be. I had him corralled just as securely as if I had built a fence round him. He couldn't travel without some sound from his dogs, and on my snowshoes I could.

I got home early the next day and for the first time since I had found Jake's body I had a feeling of security. I set out my own mink line and I wasn't worried about Klutuk, though I still covered my windows at night. I can't say I had a fine winter, but I trapped.

In the middle of April the hum of Matt's plane was a welcome sound. I had had my fur packed for several days and I was ready to go, at the lake when he touched down. We loaded my fur, rifle, snowshoes and bedroll. Klutuk was welcome to the things I had left at the cabin and I had left them there for a purpose. I wanted him to believe I'd be coming back in the fall. I knew he'd be there then, waiting for me. For now, he would have heard and seen the plane drop down from the sky. There was still plenty of snow for his dog team and not long after we took off, I knew Klutuk would be on his way to plan his stakeout.

❄ ❄ ❄

Dillingham was the same little town. The trappers hadn't started to arrive yet but the ice would be going out of the rivers soon. I worked for Tubby Griffin again, grading fur, and I found a man in town who needed a fishing partner. Henry Rhoel was an experienced fisherman and good with a sailboat. I was neither one, but Henry said all it required was hard work.

Boats began to arrive in town each day, all the men anxious to find out how much money their winter's fur catch would bring. all the men were trappers. Some of them had family with them but most had none. They had all been stricken with spring fever for the past month or so, eager to meet old friends they hadn't seen all winter and perhaps sit down with them in the restaurant bar room for a drink or two. Native men and their families came into town from as far west as Togiak. Before long, Dillingham was a small tent city.

The Trappers' Ball would take place quite soon. I had never attended one but this year I decided to go and it turned out to be quite an occasion. The movie theater in town could seat two hundred people on its wooden benches and in the summer months it was crowded every night. For the Trappers' Ball, the benches were stacked against the wall. Dillingham was cleared for action.

Red Malsbury was a local genius. If someone's radio wouldn't work and Red didn't have the part it needed, he could make something that would work. The town's two trading stores both used diesel engines to produce electricity and Red took care of those, too. He could repair any kind of machinery and he could play the piano. Red furnished the music for the Trappers' Ball and he was a master. If the glass of whiskey sitting on top of the piano had any effect on his music, nobody noticed it.

This was an occasion for dancing. All the women and girls in town, all who came from up the coast or down the big rivers, they were all there and they were kept busy. All the nurses from the Bureau of Indian Affairs Hospital, seven miles out of town, came too, except the unlucky ones who were on duty. After a few drinks even the men who couldn't dance, could and did. There was a small stage in front of the movie screen. If some of the men were overcome by too much exertion or too much drink, they were carried to the platform and laid there so as not to be trampled on. Gettogether occasions were few and far between and the Trappers' Ball was quite a time and a lot of fun.

Butch Smith was late coming down the river. Then I saw him one day, standing in front of the trading store. I went over and we sat down on the long wooden bench against the wall.

"What kind of winter did you have, Fred?"

"Well, it was kind of a strange winter, Butch. I went down the Nuyakuk to look up Jake Savolly, just as you asked me to. You were right about Klutuk. He has his camp in the Tikchiks, just about where you said he would be. I found Jake behind his cabin. He'd been shot in the back and dragged there."

For a while Butch didn't say anything but then the questions came fast. I told him the story.

"Klutuk heard the plane come in this spring and drop down. He saw it take off a little later and he knew I was leaving. There was still plenty of snow for his dog team. I'd say he was at my cabin the day after I left. Everything is still there as though I planned to be back this fall. He'll spend the summer there and he'll be waiting for me to come back. He'll be within rifleshot of the cabin."

"There's something you haven't told me."

"When I go back I'm going in to Rat Lake. You told me Harry had a cabin there. When Klutuk sees the plane drop down at Rat Lake this fall, he'll know he's wasted the summer, staking out the other cabin. But he'll know where I am. He knows that country a lot better than I do but he won't feel he's safe trying to move in on me next winter. He'll be at Rat Lake after I leave there next spring. That's when I'll have him."

"After you've left? Klutuk isn't a fool, Fred. What are you going to do?"

"He likes supplies, Butch. He cleaned out Jake's cabin, didn't even leave an empty coffee can. I left him plenty of things when I left this spring and I'm going to leave him something next spring, too. Something that won't do him too much good. They used to use a lot of strychnine along the coast here, Butch. They just about cleaned out the arctic fox with it, but they don't use it any more. I want some strychnine for the spring. Can you get it for me?"

Butch looked at me, and nodded.

"I didn't know those three surveyors Klutuk killed, but Sam Donaldson and Jake Savolly were my friends. I'll have the strychnine for you. The amount you can hold on a quarter will kill a hundred-and-fifty-pound wolf. I hope you have all the luck there is."

Henry and I went fishing. I don't think I knew what hard work was until I went salmon fishing in Bristol Bay. The wooden sailboats were thirty-two feet long, about eight feet wide and they were open. When we couldn't go any longer without rest, a series of wires and hooks enabled us to erect a small tent in the bow for shelter—but first the mast had to be taken down and the sail rolled up. When we worked, keeping the boat straight into the flood or ebb tide, several hundred feet of gill-net were paid out over the stern. No power was allowed. This was not a law. It was a condition imposed upon fishermen by the Alaskan salmon industry. There was no competition and the different companies that made up the Alaskan salmon industry agreed among themselves on the price they would pay for salmon. The name of their game was exploitation and it didn't allow men the price of an engine or fuel. Even an outboard motor would at times have saved men's lives. The sand bars in Bristol Bay were constantly shifted by the strong tides and once in a while a boat would go aground. That was the time, on the flood tide, to pray for good weather. If the tide brought a storm with it, which it often did, an open boat could swamp and men would be lost. Men's lives didn't seem to mean much, compared with the dollars of profit for the canneries.

At Bristol Bay the price was sixteen cents for each salmon. The men who fished Cook Inlet, perhaps three hundred miles east, were paid one dollar for the same kind of fish. They had competition there. It made a difference.

The canneries had skows anchored out in the bay and each fishing boat was required to report once every twenty-four hours. This ensured that the fish would be fresh and it was also a welcome break for the fishermen: after twenty-four hours of misery, we were glad to tie up to the base, glad of the hot meal we were given.

Every year a few men were lost. Every cannery had its own small cemetery with several small wooden crosses and each small cross had a man's name on it. Below the name were the words "Lost at Sea."

Henry and I had delivered a load of salmon and after we had eaten I stepped outside on the skow. I could see many white sails, some quite close, and as far as I could see there were more, all tacking against the strong wind and tide, making their way to the tally skow to deliver their fish, the men on board thinking of one thing—the hot meal waiting for them. Fishing those sailboats was a hard way to make a living but I never knew a single man to give it up of his own choice. Fishing was in their blood and it stayed there.

My first fishing season was finally over and the good success we had was to Henry's credit. I now had plenty of cash, and to spare, for my winter supplies.

The first of August I found Butch and he took me to his cabin. He gave me a pint Mason jar, almost filled with powder.

"Be careful, Fred. Klutuk is nobody's fool and he's tricky."

I told Butch I'd see him in the spring and I left him. Two days later, we loaded my things in Matt's plane and took off. In an hour we were over the Tikchik Lakes. It seemed strange to look at that beautiful country and know that there was a killer there. I knew Klutuk was waiting for me at the foot of the first lake. He was going to be angry and puzzled when the plane flew over and didn't land. He was going to know, when he saw the plane drop down over Rat Lake, that his long summer's wait for me had been wasted, that all he had gained were the supplies I had left behind. He was going to know what I would do to his traps. Getting me would have to be postponed for another year.

We set down on Rat Lake and the cabin there was in good shape; it had a wide overhang, like a big shed roof, on the front. We unloaded everything and I told Matt to pick me up the first of March. He took out his notebook and wrote the pickup date in it. To some trappers the pickup time was important and it was to me, this time. I wanted Klutuk still to have plenty of good dog-team weather after I left in the spring. I wanted him at Rat Lake then.

I watched as Matt gunned his motor and rose from the lake. I knew Klutuk was watching too. Matt made one circle over me and dipped his wings, then headed back for the coast.

I had a feeling of frustration. I was in a wonderful fur country yet knowledge of Klutuk's presence had me pretty well pinned down. The fact that I thought I had him under control didn't help much. Till the snows came most of my time was taken by watching and listening.

Harry Stevens had been a capable man. His cabins were well equipped, with plenty of hand-hewn shelves for storage space. I spent the next few days putting up enough wood for the winter. I had brought a swede saw with me this time. It was nothing more than a steel bow fitted with a thin narrow blade, but it could cut through logs with no more sound than a slight whisper. I didn't want to be in a position where I was prevented from hearing the smallest sound. I knew I had Klutuk more or less on the defensive, but he was a dangerous antagonist. Five dead men told me that.

Harry Stevens had built his main cabin at the junction of Rat Creek and the Tikchik River, Butch had told me. Harry had used a dog team himself to travel with in winter. He had trapped this area and he had well-brushed trails on all the creeks and along the main river. I followed his trail down the creek one day and it brought me to the main cabin. It was built just a short distance from the river, big and comfortable. When I stepped inside it, I wished I could winter there.

Harry had made a chair with a sloping back so that he could sit at ease by the stove and relax. There was the usual stack of stove wood against one of the log walls and a pile of dry shavings. Everything was ready for him, whenever he came back. It was an odd feeling, to realize that Harry wasn't coming back. As Butch had said, anything could have happened to him.

I didn't hang around long. I knew that until the snow came there was always the chance that I might have company I didn't want. When winter came, I'd have Klutuk under control. He couldn't bring his dogs too close for they always make a sound. When dogs travel, they bark once in a while; even when they are tied up there is always an occasional howl or yelp. So now, in the evenings, after it was dark and I had put my lamp out, I would sit in the open doorway of my cabin and listen to the night sounds. A sharp pop on the lake meant a beaver, slapping his broad tail on the water as he dove under. A short grunt or two, on the other side of the small lake, told me a moose was there, feeding on lily pads. Once in a while, a coughing bellow told me a grizzly was around, upset and angry about something, as they always are. I had seen several places on Rat Creek where they had hauled salmon from the water, so I knew there were plenty of them close by.

In early November I set out a short string of mink traps on Rat Creek, enough to make me feel I was doing something. The only recent close encounter I'd had with a grizzly had been the one that had jumped me the previous fall. I still hadn't the experience I needed to make me aware of the real danger they presented.

I was on the trail going down Rat Creek, early one morning, and I met a grizzly coming the other way, no more than fifty feet off. He stopped and raised his front feet off the ground a little, looking me over. His lips rolled back and a growl came from deep in his throat. I fired just as he dropped back down on his feet, and it seemed a clean miss. He walked toward me slowly and I fired into his chest. He stopped and another shot went into the same place. He dropped then, and after a few moments I was sure he was dead and walked over to him. The first shot I had fired had barely grazed his shoulder but the next two shots were in the center of his chest, no more than two inches apart.

The weather turned cold. It meant meat would keep now and it was no problem getting a moose. Finally, the first heavy snowfall came and there was plenty of it; when it stopped and the days were clear and cold, I believe there was three feet of snow. Now I could feel safe, but all the same I went over my strategy for penning up Klutuk every day and every night, reasoning out my theory over and again, and reasoning out his responses whenever I paused, whenever I heard an unexpected sound.

Mink were the big fur catch in that area and they traveled the main Tikchik river and the small creeks that emptied into it. I moved some supplies down to Harry's main cabin and stayed there several days at a time. My snowshoe trail followed the river, not Harry's trail; it was hard-packed and easy to travel on and it suited me better. One day as I was traveling up the river I heard a slight sound behind me, and looked back. Where my trail had been was a ten-foot stretch of black, rolling water: the ice under my hard-packed trail had been worn away by the current and tested too far by my passage. I walked straight for the river bank. Harry's brushed-out dog-team trails were a lot safer. I was young then but I should have given some thought to why Harry had worked so hard to brush out trails, when he had the nice frozen river to travel on. I knew now why he had done it and I never again used the river to travel on. Little by little, I was learning how to survive.

Spring arrived and the first of March wasn't far away. I began to make my set for Klutuk. The swede saw I had was only two feet long and handy to use. I knew he'd want it. There were plenty of beaver along Rat Creek and I knew he'd be after them, so I picked out some nice number four beaver traps and put them with the saw.

I had a small glass jar fitted with a screw top. I measured two teaspoons of sugar into it. I poured strychnine on a quarter, all it would hold, and dumped that in the jar, too, and I kept that up until the jar was full. I still used the same tin tea can. It had been used to make tea or coffee over an open fire many times and it was burned black, the way it should be. Nothing to rouse suspicion. I placed the jar of treated sugar inside it and nestled a small cloth bag of tea round it. It was just the thing I would carry in my pack and I knew Klutuk would too. I hung the can, the small swede saw and the beaver traps from the overhang in front of the cabin and waited anxious days for Matt to arrive.

One evening, just at dusk, I heard a distant rifle shot. It came from Klutuk's direction. He had probably taken a caribou. Sound travels far when it is cold and still and that shot must have been twenty miles away. So far, my plan was working. I still remembered the way Jake Savolly had looked when I found him. What I had placed in the small tin can was my gift to Klutuk.

❅ ❅ ❅

On the first of March I heard a hum in the distance and then there was a small speck in the sky. Matt would be here in about twenty minutes. His ski plane pulled almost up to the cabin door. We loaded my fur and rifle and a few more things and I climbed aboard.

"You have a good winter, Fred?"

"Just fair, Matt. How are things in town?"

"Same old way. Nothing much changes there in the winter time. You knew Kid Wilkins? Well, he cut his foot pretty bad this winter. His axe slipped. They brought him down the river by dog team but by the time they got him to hospital, infection had got so bad it was up in his hip. They couldn't save him."

Matt's plane was an old Waco. He started the motor by turning a crank that folded back into the cowling. After he got the crank whirling fast enough, something grabbed hold inside and the motor would start off with a cough and then go into a beautiful steady roar. It was a biplane and Matt could make that old crate do things that planes aren't supposed to do. He was a wonderful pilot. He told me that he and Lindbergh had attended the same flying school at the same time.

There was a small lake in Dillingham and Matt landed there. As we unloaded my things I saw a man coming down the hill on snowshoes and he was hurrying. When he got to us, he held his hand out to me.

"I'm Carlos Larson, the local game warden. Got to keep an eye on you boys."

"What are you looking for?"

"Oh, a man can never tell, you know. Have a good winter?"

"Fair."

"Not much fur?"

"Some."

"Say, just where do you trap?"

"The Tikchiks."

"What I mean is, just where is your cabin? What lake?"

"It's a small lake, Larson. You couldn't find it. I don't think it has a name."

"Oh. Well, I'll see you around."

He left then and headed back up the hill. I turned to Matt, my face one big question. He grinned.

"You didn't hear Larson ask me where I picked you up. He knows I won't fly him anywhere and I never tell him where I take a man. There's a pilot here in town who flies for Larson. They'll fly the Tikchiks in the winter months and they'll finally spot your snowshoe trails and follow them to your cabin. Larson just never gives up."

"Why in the world would he want to find my cabin?"

"Maybe you get your moose at the wrong time of year. Perhaps you trap mink when the season is closed. Larson loves to find someone like that. He'll be looking for you."

"Well, I take my moose when the weather gets cold enough and I trap mink when they seem to be running loose. I think I'll keep on doing that."

I carried my fur to the trading store and told Tubby I'd give him a hand buying fur after the trappers started to come in.

I went to my cabin then and got the oil stove going, pulling a chair up close. I sat there for a while, letting the place warm up. I thought of Togiak and the year I had spent there. I thought of last year and poor old Jake Savolly and I thought of the winter just past and the one to come.

By the middle of May the first riverboats had arrived and from then on it was an everyday thing. The restaurant was filled with trappers now, the liquor store was busy and things were back to what was a normal spring for Dillingham. Every spring seemed to be the same in another way, too. There was always someone who said, "I stopped by Pete's place on the way down. Been nobody there for a long time." Or it might be Tom's place, or Mike's place. There was always someone who didn't show up. It might have been a grizzly in the fall or perhaps someone had dropped through the ice. I had almost done that, but I'd been lucky.

I was having supper in the restaurant one night when Red Vale came in and sat by me.

"Fred, you knew Carl Taylor didn't you?"

Everyone knew Carl Taylor and yet no one knew him too well. He was a very quiet man, always pleasant, but he kept pretty much to himself. He didn't fish, he worked in the cannery in town among a hundred other people and that let him be alone, the way he wanted it.

Red continued: "Carl's cabin is about eight miles below mine. On my way down the river, I stopped by his place. The door was open but the place was still warm and there was a fire going in the stove. Carl wore house slippers round the cabin. I followed his fresh footprints in the snow and he'd gone to the river. He'd chopped his water hole bigger, big enough so he could step through it, and I guess that's what he did. There were no tracks coming back. I went back to his cabin and looked around. There was a bible open on the table and a place underlined in pencil. It read 'The time is now.' The open pages were telling about the second coming, the second coming of Christ. I guess Carl couldn't wait, Fred. He had to go and meet Him and maybe he did. I hope he did."

Butch Smith was late getting down the river again. He wasn't in a hurry any more. He was getting old enough now so he could look back and see a long, winding trail behind him and he could look ahead and almost see the end of it. I was getting older every year too, but I didn't feel any older. I learned something every year and there was plenty for me to learn.

He came in one evening; he had arrived in town that afternoon.

"What kind of winter, Fred?"

"Waiting, watching and listening. There's good fur in there but I haven't really been able to go after it."

"Klutuk?"

"He's still there. I heard a rifle shot at dusk about the middle of February. He's still in the same place."

"You did something with the stuff I gave you?"

"I've set a trap for him and I think I'll have him. It wasn't something I wanted to do but when I think of Jake Savolly and the shape he was in when I found him, I've got no bad feeling about it. If Klutuk had the chance, he'd shoot me like a dog."

I went fishing again with Henry Rhoel and learned some more. The only deck on a sailboat was a small area on the sloping bow big enough to hold an anchor and a large coil of anchor rope. These were made fast with a tie rope that ran through a cleat. The deck surface was always wet and it was always slippery. A small guard rail round the bow would have helped but no one could afford refinements. When it was necessary to throw the anchor overboard or to pull it in, you were on your hands and knees, very careful that no part of your body was in that coil of rope, for it went over the side like a whipping snake.

The centerboard was a large, flat wooden plate that was lowered through the bottom of the boat to keep it from drifting or, in rough weather, to prevent it from capsizing. The housing for the centerboard ran from the bow toward the stern for a distance of ten feet, the same height as the sides of the boat and six inches wide. When it was necessary to raise the mast, you had to walk this narrow housing with the mast on your shoulder. The end of the mast was rounded to fit into a hole, called the step, in the solid base fixed in the bottom of the boat. When you walked forward and slotted the base of the mast in this hole, you were stepping the mast. That done, you continued to walk forward, allowing the mast to slide over your shoulder until it was upright. Four feet from the bottom of the boat and fastened to the center edge of the small bow was a metal collar. This had to be placed round the mast and held in place by dropping an iron pin through a slot provided for it. In rough weather, this could be a dangerous procedure. The heavy weight on your shoulder might cause you to lose your balance and go down: instead of falling to the bottom of the boat, you'd be thrown over the side. Several men had lost their lives this way.

That second year I fished in Bristol Bay I had first-hand experience of the dangers that constantly faced the men who worked the wooden sailboats.

Henry and I had delivered our load of salmon to the skow, eaten the welcome hot meal and I had stepped outside. It was a clear day, with a nice brisk wind that meant good sailing weather.

Ray Blatchford and Billy Hurd came out of the cook shack and, as I watched, Ray climbed down into their boat. I saw Billy step down on to the small sloping bow and all in a moment his foot slipped and I heard his shout as he went over the side. Ray ran to the stern and I saw Billy's head as the strong current swept him along the side of the boat. One of his hands grabbed the end of a tie rope trailing from the stern and Ray bent down and reached for his wrist.

I was standing on the walkway along the side of the skow, holding on to the heavy safety rope. I saw Ray's reaching hand barely touch Billy's wrist and he was gone. I was close enough to hear Ray when he said, "Billy, why didn't you hang on?"

He stared at the railing rope as though he might see Billy's hand there. He straightened up and climbed the side of the skow and stood beside me. I stared down at the dark, cold water and saw the flash of a yellow oilskin as the current threw Billy to the surface, and then there was nothing.

Ray's voice was soft as he said, "Billy knew he shouldn't step down on the bow. He just wasn't thinking." He turned away and went back into the cook shack. He wouldn't fish any more that season. Billy's wife would be paid the average amount of money earned by the fishermen and Ray would be paid the same. One more white cross would be placed in the small cannery cemetery and it would have Billy's name on it.

Henry came out and his face told me he knew what had happened.

"Where to, Fred?"

"Let's get out of here. Head across the bay and try the Ekwok rip tides."

We climbed down into our boat, Henry untied the rope that held us fast to the skow and the current took us away. I hauled down on the rope and tackle and our sail rose up to the top of the mast, taut and snapping in the wind. Henry ducked down as the boom swung round in a sharp arc and passed above him. He pulled hard on the rudder and we tacked straight into the wind.

Billy Hurd's death was something I couldn't ignore or just push out of my mind. I was glad when the season was over. I didn't stay in Dillingham long. I got my supplies together and I bought a new, bolt-action Winchester rifle. It was a .30–06, the same caliber as the old army Springfield I had been carrying, but I wanted a rifle I knew I could depend on. I'd had two encounters with grizzlies and I knew there would be more. This summer, too, I thought I'd be free to use the creeks and rivers without fear of wondering who might be stalking me from cover or the banks. I wanted a canoe. While I was looking around for one, word came into town that a man named John Shipton had jumped off the dock at the Nushagak cannery, across the bay. He had been wearing hip boots and had pulled them off, jumped off the dock and swum to shore. He was last seen running up the bank of the Nushagak. He had friends who organized an air search for him but no trace had been found. That had been the first week in June. It was early August now. He had been gone a long time.

I found the canoe I wanted and Matt flew me out of Dillingham. We landed on Rat Lake, taxiing up close to the cabin. I took my rifle and climbed out. From where I was standing I could see that the things I had left for Klutuk were gone.

"Matt, wait for a few minutes. I'll be right back."

I walked to the cabin and checked to be sure. The saw, traps and tea can were gone. I opened the cabin door, if Klutuk had taken anything else it hadn't been much.

I stepped outside and stood there, trying to put things together. I couldn't believe that Klutuk would spend the summer here and touch nothing. I knew he wore *mukluks*. Like moccasins, they don't leave much trace but even so he couldn't have walked through the moss and dry leaves that covered the ground in front of the cabin and not have left some trace, and I could find no sign of him there.

If things hadn't looked right I had intended to climb back into Matt's plane and circle the area until I found Klutuk's camp. I'd become the hunter then, for I'd made up my mind that I would run no more. I walked over to Matt.

"Let's get her unloaded."

It didn't take us long. We piled everything in front of the cabin and covered it with a light tarpaulin I brought from the cabin. The canoe we carried away from the shore and I told Matt to pick me up in the middle of May, if the weather held cold enough. If not, I'd be waiting for him whenever he came in.

Matt left and I stood for a little while. Then I picked up my rifle and crossed Rat Creek, just below the mouth, where it left the lake. There were plenty of beaver on the creek and I knew Klutuk would have been after them that spring. The timber was fairly heavy and moss was thick on the ground. I walked with no sound at all and watched the other side of the creek. After two miles of slow walking I saw patches of white on the other side. I moved in closer to the creek and saw that they were pieces of faded canvas. It had been a tent and I knew it had been Klutuk's.

I crossed to the other side and his campsite was a debris of scattered equipment. The bears had been there. The tent was in pieces, a small dog sled was turned on its side. I looked around and found where five dogs had been chained but there was no sign of them having starved or any bones that would tell me the bears had killed them. Like a lot of other men, Klutuk had turned his dogs loose to travel with him. It's a good insurance against being surprised by a bear—dogs will never range too far from the man they are with. He had cut a branch from a spruce tree, leaving a piece of the limb for a hanger, and my saw and traps were there. A .30–30 rifle was lying on the ground and dozens of rounds of ammunition were scattered round about. There was plenty of .22 ammunition, too, but no rifle. He had taken that with him. My tea can was lying to one side. The cover was gone and it was empty. I spotted the small glass jar but the lid was still screwed on. Fear clutched me for a moment. Could this all be an elaborate trap? Tense, I walked over to the jar and picked it up. Some of the contents had been used. I laid the jar back on the ground. I would bury it later. Slowly I walked down the trail. Not more than three hundred yards from the campsite I found him. He had been there since early spring. He had been a small man, not much over five feet tall. His .22 rifle was there and I left it with him.

I went back to his camp. His .30–30 rifle had a front sight that had been carved from ivory and it was a beautiful job. I knocked it out of its slot with the handle of my hunting knife. It was the only souvenir I wanted, and it wasn't for me. I walked back to the lake and sat in the open doorway of my cabin.

Two years of being hunted were over. I had no remorse and yet I wasn't easy in my mind. It was strange to have killed a man and then to look upon him for the first time. Somewhere I had read that man-hunting was the king of sports. I hadn't found it that way.

I took a few things to eat from under the tarp, and sat down again in the open doorway. Somehow I was tired and I sat there a long time, looking out over the lake. When dusk came I saw a cow moose wandering along on the other side of the lake. She had her calf with her and I wondered if she was the same one that had hung around there last fall. I finally went inside and lit the lamp, and for the first time in two years I didn't cover the windows. I sat at the table reading a book, trying to get my mind on to something else.

A tap-tap-tap on the window across the cabin caused a stillness in my heart. I was twenty-eight years old and didn't have a nerve in my body but I couldn't stop a small shiver that tried to crawl up my spine. Klutuk? I had seen Klutuk that day and he hadn't looked as though he'd be tapping on my window. And yet . . . I grabbed a flashlight from the table and went to the window. Nothing. I went back to my book but it was hard to focus on it. Tap, tap, tap . . . came on the window, my side this time. I turned my head deliberately, not too anxious to see what was there. A mink sat on the window ledge. He tapped the windowpane again and disappeared into the darkness.

I slept well that night. When I woke, the morning was bright, the sun just breaking over the mountaintops. I started a fire in the stove and stepped outside. A loud hiss, above my head, made me move quickly and I looked up. A mink sat on a log above the door, and I could see two long porcupine quills deeply embedded in its head. That explained its strange behavior the night before. I went back inside, brought out my .22 and shot it.

I fixed something for breakfast and after I had eaten I went down Rat Creek to bury the glass jar and cover Klutuk's bones.

I had been in the Tikchiks nearly three years, and for the first time I knew complete freedom. I worked hard that winter, spending much of my time at Harry Stevens' cabin on the Tikchik. I made a good fur catch but by the middle of April I couldn't wait to hear the hum of Matt's plane. Once in a while that winter, I'd realized I was still listening. It had been impossible to push Klutuk completely from my mind.

When Matt arrived he had to have his usual cup of coffee, then he helped me load my things. We got into Dillingham that afternoon and I took my fur to Tubby. I'd had all I wanted of running the liquor store but I told him I'd buy fur for him when he needed me.

Later, much later, in May, I saw Butch sitting at the counter in the restaurant. I went in, slid a stool next to him and sat down. When he shook my hand, there was a question in his eyes.

I reached in my pocket and took out a piece of crumpled paper. I took from it the small ivory sight and placed it in his hand.

"Klutuk carried a thirty–thirty, Butch. He won't need it any more."

He looked at me and nodded his head, then he dropped the ivory sight into his shirt pocket.

"Fred, I know you don't drink much but I'd like to buy you one."

Butch was around for several years after that. His wife died and he eventually went to the Pioneers' Home in Sitka, and he passed away there. Butch was never a man to talk much, and I know the story of Klutuk stayed with him.

The legend of Klutuk lived for a long time. People wondered where he had gone. There were some who thought he must have gone to the Kuskokwim area and, in a way, they were right. The Stony River flowed into the Kuskokwim and Klutuk's camp had been close to the Stony.

I was twenty-eight years old when I caused Klutuk's death. That was a long time ago, and to this day I have no regrets. I'm sorry, of course, that it had to happen, but I simply had no choice.

5 / John Shipton

Henry and I fished together again, and the summer passed slowly for me. For the first time I could look forward to a year in the Tikchiks, with no one to worry about, and I was eager to go back. In the middle of August Matt and I loaded my supplies in his plane, and we left Dillingham.

We landed on Rat Lake and unloaded everything. It was late in the afternoon and like the previous year we just placed all the boxes and sacks in one pile in front of the cabin and spread a light waterproof tarp over everything. I knew I'd have plenty of time in the morning to get all my supplies stowed away.

I told Matt to pick me up at the beginning of April and, just the way it was every fall when he left, he was soon only a small dot above the horizon. I took a few things from the stack of supplies, enough for supper, and sat in the open cabin door for quite a while. It was a new feeling for me, to feel free and easy.

I slept well that night and I was up at daybreak. I stepped outside the cabin and walked to my pile of supplies and threw off the tarp. I don't know whether I heard a voice, or just a sound.

73

I turned and saw a man's head perhaps twenty feet away. The hair was long and matted and the face was bearded, and it was framed by the willow brush that was hiding the body I couldn't see. I don't know how to describe the feeling that was in me. His eyes were sunken and hollow and I knew I was looking at a man who was starved. Finally, I nodded my head.

"Why don't you come out?"

He pushed his way through the brush, and stood there.

"You know who I am?"

"No. No, I don't."

"I'm John Shipton. You thought I was dead, didn't you?"

John Shipton. It rang a bell in my mind. He was the man who had jumped off the dock at Nushagak in the spring.

I don't know how he had the strength to stand. His feet were bare, cut and swollen. His pants and shirt were shreds of cloth, hanging on him. He looked to me like a man who just might run again and I didn't want that.

"I don't know you, John, I never saw you before. You're hungry. Come over here and we'll find something to eat, and I'll find something for your feet. I'll bet they hurt."

He moved over to me slowly, and stood there. I found a small sack of oatmeal and handed it to him. I knew I had a grown-up child on my hands. He had been a big man; he was skin and bones now. I found my winter pants and underwear in the pile, and beckoned. He followed me into the cabin and I had him sit on the bunk. I put a pan of water on the stove to heat. I would soak his feet in that and I put another small pot of water on for the oatmeal.

"You don't know me. I'm Fred Hatfield. I've lived in this country three years. I think this water is warm enough for your feet. Take your clothes off and put these on."

His body was surprisingly clean but I guess he had been in enough rivers and creeks to make it that way. He put my long underwear on and I got his feet into the pan of warm water, adding a little disinfectant. When I gave him a cup of oatmeal gruel to drink he threw it up at once, but the second cupful stayed down, and I made him drink some more. He puzzled me. He had a worried expression on his face and his eyes looked haunted. I cleaned the cuts in his feet and dried them off with a towel.

"John, you know me now. I want you to lie down on the bunk and cover up. You need lots of rest. I'll step outside and it will be quiet in here."

He lay back on the bunk and I covered him with blankets.

"Fred?"

"Yes?"

"Will you keep watch?"

"Keep watch for what?"

"So nobody will come."

"I'll keep watch. No one will come." I stepped outside. "I'll leave the door open. If you want me, just call."

I walked the short distance to the lake shore and sat down. I knew I had John on my hands. It was going to take several days to get him in shape and that would be just the beginning. The clothes he had on were my winter clothing. All of this meant just one thing. John and I would be going down these rivers in a canoe and we had to go soon. It would be a trip out to the coast, to Dillingham, and riding those wild rivers in a canoe wouldn't be a pleasure trip. After I got John on his feet and in shape to travel, there would be many days on the rivers. Before long there could be skim ice on the water and if we didn't move soon it would mean waiting all winter. I almost began to believe this big lake country had a curse on me.

My big problem was the fact that I didn't know any of the rivers. It would be a slow, careful trip. Two hours went by and I sat there, batting a mosquito once in a while. There wasn't much for me to think about. I knew what we had to do. It was just a matter of waiting for John to get in shape to travel. And persuading him to come with me.

"Fred?"

"Coming."

I went to the cabin. He was sitting on the edge of the bunk.

"You didn't leave me, did you, Fred?"

"No. I told you I'd be outside."

I warmed more water for his feet and had him soak them once more.

"John, I'm going to make a batch of hot cakes. You need lots to eat and I'll bet you're hungry."

"Yes, I am, Fred, I'm really hungry."

If John would eat ten times a day I'd feed him ten times a day. I wanted him to get some flesh on his bones and I wanted his feet to get well.

"How far did you go this summer, John?"

"I got as far as the Kuskokwim. I came out near Sleet-mute but I didn't go in to the village."

"Why not? Why didn't you go in?"

"They're still after me, Fred. Do you know why I jumped off the dock at Nushagak? Do you know why I ran up the river?"

"No, I sure don't."

"There were four men coming down the dock. Three of them carried a timber and one of them had a coil of rope. They were going to hang me, Fred."

I knew the men with the timbers and rope had been going to work to straighten up the pipeline that carried water to the cannery. That was a springtime job for all the canneries.

"John, I think they were just going to work some-where."

"No, Fred, they were going to hang me."

I knew I was in deep water so I didn't try any more. "Eat your hot cakes, John." I watched him for a minute. "You had a long trip to the Kuskokwim. That's quite a ways."

"The wolves almost had me one time, Fred. They were circled all around me."

It wouldn't have done any good to tell him that wolves always check everything, and John was a stranger in their country. He obviously had a mind of his own and nothing could change it. I had no idea in the world what had made him the way he was. Every small sound was a danger and a threat to John. His next sentence startled me, though.

"Fred, I know where there's lots of gold."

I had to ask him where.

"It's about forty miles from here, maybe. I came to a small valley and there was a big outcropping of rose quartz on both sides of it. The gold was in the quartz like ribbons."

"Where did you cross the Tikchik?"

"Just below the canyon."

I knew where that canyon was. If John had gone the way he said he had, his valley would be about five miles west of the headwaters of the King Salmon. He had been very close to Klutuk's camp and John would never know how lucky he was that Klutuk's bones were buried on Rat Creek.

There *was* gold on the King Salmon, fine gold from the grass roots to thirty feet down. A glacier had put it in there but there was no concentration. Men had looked for the source for a long time and it sounded as though John might have found it. If his mind got straightened out and he came back in with me next year, we could have a try for it. If he didn't, I could go after it myself. It was all open tundra country and the valley shouldn't be difficult to find.

I dried John's feet and in minutes he was sound asleep. I went outside again and sat down and watched the night sky for a time. Later, as I made up a bed on the cabin floor, I fell asleep thinking about our trip down those wild rivers.

It took ten days for John's feet to heal and then he was able to wear my winter boots. His frame had filled out and he looked a new man but his mind was still in a strange world. I had asked him how he had found his way around all summer.

"If I came to a straight stick I knew that was the way I was supposed to go. The way it was pointing."

"Is that the way you found Sleetmute?"

"Oh, no, I wasn't looking for Sleetmute. I came to a creek and there were men working gold claims there. It was Bear Creek. One of the men gave me some shoes and one of them gave me a hat, but I lost them. They told me to follow down the creek and it would take me to Sleetmute, and it did."

"What did you eat all the time you were gone?"

"Willow buds and cranberries."

When I had walked out of Togiak in the spring of 1936 I had chewed on a lot of willow buds and they are not tasty. No wonder John had got skinny. I wondered how to break the news to him of our trip and wondered how I'd handle him on the water if he acted up.

"John, can you use a canoe?"

"I used one a lot on the Mulchatna."

My dad had just about raised me in a canoe and knowing that John was handy with one made me feel better.

"John, you want to spend the winter with me, don't you?"

"You won't make me leave, will you?"

"You know better than that. It's just that we need a lot of things. You're wearing my winter pants, my shirt and my winter boots. You're wearing all my winter clothing. The only place we can get these things is in Dillingham. That means a canoe trip out to the coast. Will you go with me?"

John stared at me, a look of fear in his eyes.

"You wouldn't leave me there, Fred?"

"No, John, I won't leave you."

I could see the uncertainty and doubt that were in him. Then he said, "I'll go with you."

Getting ready to leave was just a matter of putting a few supplies in the canoe. Everything else we carried into the cabin and stacked it on the floor, for we'd be moving down to the main cabin on the river when we came back. That evening we were sitting by the cabin door, talking about the trip ahead. There was a loud slap on the water and John was on the alert at once.

"Fred, that's the men from Wood River. They're here."

John was obsessed with a fear that there were men after him, men who were hunting for him. Wood River was a long way off; it drained a chain of lakes and entered the Nushagak ten miles above Dillingham. I had never tried to question John about his past life on the Mulchatna. All I knew was that he had lived there and trapped there and now he lived in a world of fear, a world of fantasy that I hadn't been able to penetrate.

I got my flashlight. "Let's go and see what it is."

We walked to the lake shore and I held the light on the water. Before long a beaver swam into its circle and I snapped it off, and on again. There was a loud slap from his broad tail as he dived.

"Now you know, John. It was just a beaver."

We left early the next morning and the few miles of Rat Creek were nice going. We entered the Tikchik. This and all the rivers beyond us would be new water to me. The Tikchik was a fast river and some of the rapids were rough. A sudden bend might show a sweeper just below us and we had to watch for that. Where the current had undercut the bank a tree might have tumbled into the water, its base still held fast by strong roots. The rest of the tree would extend out into the river and could sweep the men in a canoe into the water.

It was a relief when we entered Nuyakuk Lake: ten miles of smooth going and then we were at the foot of the lake, and the head of the Nuyakuk river was there. This was where I had spent my first winter and I decided to take advantage of the shelter that cabin would give, and stay overnight. I had covered the first fifteen miles of the Nuyakuk when I had looked for Jake Savolly, and I knew the water was rough. We could use a night's rest before we started downriver.

It was something new for me to know that there was no one in this country now who might have his rifle lined up on my back. This time I had other worries. Soon after daybreak we set off, keeping fairly close to the river bank. I don't know how many times I heard rapids ahead or saw them.

"Pull for the shore, John, pull hard." He always did.

I knew about the twenty-foot fall before we came to Jake's cabin, and we carried the canoe around that. The cabin couldn't be seen from the river and I didn't tell John it was there. Jake's bones were still the way I had found them and that would have been all John needed to get him completely upset, so we kept on going.

Grizzlies seemed to be everywhere. It was easy to understand why extreme caution was needed if you traveled a river trail. So many rapids and forced carries didn't help to make good time. We made camp five nights on the Nuyakuk and hit the Nushagak on the sixth day. This river was wide and deep, still free of ice, and we made good time. We were on the main travel route now, and we passed several riverboats, all of them heading up, all of them trappers going to their winter homes.

After four more days we reached the small river village of Ekwok. The people there knew John and were glad to see him, but he stayed pretty close to me. None of them talked to him about him running off that spring. We spent the night there and next morning they put a big skiff in the water and tied our canoe on a line from the stern. Their outboard motor made fast time down the river and we reached Dillingham that afternoon. From the time we left Rat Lake, we had been gone twelve days.

We carried the canoe up to the trading store with us and set it to one side, out of the way. Tubby Griffin walked over, staring with a blank expression on his face.

"John, you know Tubby don't you? Tubby, we need some things, mostly clothing for me and John."

I walked with him to his corner office and we sat down.

"Fred, where did you find him?"

"I think John found me. He's a little mixed up, so don't ask him about things. We'll be here the first thing in the morning and get what we need."

We left the store then and went to the restaurant. The boys from Ekwok had spread the word and the place was crowded. The cook was the bartender and the drinks were on the house. This was a chance for celebration and they had no intention of passing it up. No one was funny with John. They had all seen men with cabin fever and, I guess, a few who had gone bush happy. John must have been slapped on the shoulder fifty times.

"Good old John." "Good to see you, John." "Glad you're back, John."

The whiskey flowed freely and it flowed in water glasses. John and I had coffee and some food to eat. I don't think anyone noticed when we left and walked toward my cabin. Being in town this way had made a difference to John. When we got inside he asked me if I had been very far north of Rat Lake.

"I found a cabin about twenty miles north of there, Fred. It's on the timberline and it's good marten country. There's a small lake there, big enough for a plane to land on."

"Is the cabin in good shape?"

"It needs a new roof."

Marten were worth seventy dollars apiece then and I think that made my mind up for me.

"How far from the Tikchik River, John?"

"Not more than a mile."

That was all I needed to know. It was good marten country and the river, I knew, was alive with mink.

"We'll talk with Matt in the morning. If he knows where that little lake is, we'll give it a try."

Morning came too soon. I was still tired, for the trip down the rivers had been hard, but we couldn't waste a day more than we had to. After we had breakfast, we went to Matt's place.

"John, tell Matt as close as you can where that old cabin is, and the lake it's on."

When John described the location, Matt nodded. "I've flown over that area several times, Fred, and I can set you down there. If you want marten, that's the place to go to. They like to hang around the timberline and that's where you'll be."

"We've got a lot of things to get together, Matt. If you can drive your pickup to the trading store in about two hours, we'll be ready."

A cabin with the roof caved in, as John had described it, meant we needed many things I hadn't had to have before. We needed a Yukon stove and panes of glass for windows. We needed hinges, for I had an idea that the old cabin would need a new door too.

John needed a complete outfit of clothing for the winter. He insisted he had to have a twelve-gauge, automatic shotgun as well and I gave in to him. He still thought he needed protection. Matt picked us up and before long everything was loaded on his plane, our canoe tied to the top of one of the floats.

We passed over the Wood River Lakes and then we were over the Tikchiks. John pointed down to the second lake. He seemed to have changed for the better. He talked about things now.

"I crossed that lake on my way through here."

"How did you get across?"

"I found a dry drift log and used it for a float. I swam across. Fred, there are more grizzlies in here than any other place in Alaska. You'll have to keep your eyes open." I could see the tundra was dotted with them.

We set down on a small lake not more than a hundred yards from the timberline. Beyond that was open tundra as far as I could see. Matt made the plane fast to shore and we unloaded. All three of us followed a dim trail and fifty yards along we found the cabin. It was old but the walls looked solid and were standing straight. John had been right about the roof; all the old split logs and a foot of sod were piled up in the center of the floor. I guessed it had been built long before Harry Stevens' time. Perhaps another trapper had come in here from the Kuskokwim: looking north I could see part of the Kuskokwim range.

"Matt, do you think you can fly over to Rat Lake and pick up the supplies we left there? You'll find everything in the middle of the cabin floor."

He lifted from the water and left us. The little lake was perhaps a thousand yards long and he had plenty of room for his takeoff.

John and I started to throw out all the loose timber and sod. In two hours Matt was back from Rat Lake with all the things we had left there. We needed the shovel and axes for the work ahead of us.

"Matt, pick us up in the middle of April. We'll be looking for you."

"I'll be here." He shook hands with us.

We got to work then and soon the old cabin floor was clear. John was good with an axe. He split logs, ten inches in diameter, and we soon had the roof shaped up. Plenty of moss and a good foot of sod over that and it was done. We cleaned the remnants of old moss from between the logs and rechinked them, tamping fresh moss solidly into the cracks.

We explored the pale green lake and found that it contained northern pike. The northern pike is a bony fish but some of these were monsters, almost like young alligators: I saw duck and muskrat swimming along and a sudden swirl in the water marked the end of them. A small creek drained the lake and had nice trout in it, so we wouldn't go hungry. We had seen several moose, but the weather was too warm for meat to keep well.

John had brought in an extra suit of winter underwear with him but he wouldn't wear it. Someone had done something to it, he told me. He worked for some time making two pieces of U-shaped wood. These he spiked on either side of the door inside the cabin. Painstakingly, he fashioned a piece of wood almost four inches square to fit across the door like a solid bar. John was on guard again against intruders. He came to me one day; there was something he had to show me. Down the trail, thirty feet from the cabin, he pointed to the ground.

"Fred, I've got six of those big number four traps set here. They'll stop anyone who tries to get to us."

Those traps were big and each jaw carried several sharp teeth. I believe they would have held a grizzly for a while. I marked the spot well in my mind and avoided that part of the trail.

It was the beginning of October now and other than being in good physical shape, John, suddenly, was almost as he had been when I first found him.

I went to the small creek that drained our lake and brought six fat trout back to the cabin. I cleaned them and laid them across a log for our supper that night. Later, when I went to get them, they were gone.

"John, did you see the trout I laid here?"

"Yes, Fred. They had been poisoned and I threw them in the brush."

I knew John was getting away from me. I tried every thing I could think of. I took him on long hikes across the tundra but he would sit down and insist on telling me all over again about the men who were after him. Early in November he came to me.

"Fred, I'm going to have to leave you."

This was something I didn't believe even John would contemplate.

"John, aren't we trapping partners?"

"Yes."

"Then you can't leave me."

"I'm worried about my friends on the Mulchatna, Fred. They're wondering where I am."

"They know where you are. They know you're with me. We'll be getting snow before long. The Mulchatna is at least a hundred and fifty miles from here, maybe a lot more. If you try it, John, you have a long trail ahead of you. You can't make it that far."

I couldn't stop him. Next morning he started to get ready so I gave in and made him take the things I knew he would need, food that would last, extra wool socks, his shotgun and a bedroll of blankets. I tied a pair of snowshoes on his packboard. He'd be needing them before long. We shook hands and wished each other luck.

I watched him as he climbed the small hill by the lake. He reached the top and I thought he might turn and wave but he didn't. John's mind was somewhere else now. I guess I said a little prayer for him. There was nothing else I could do. I knew he'd never make it but I hoped for a miracle.

I took up the traps he had hidden so carefully on the trail. He had been a strange man but he had meant something to me. I had always had hope that I could get his mind straightened out; maybe if he had stayed with me, I could have. Having John with me had been like having something for a while, and then not having it. I had found him when he was starving to death and for all his strange ways, I knew I would miss him.

* * *

There was a game trail along the timberline. Moose and grizzlies, wolverine and fox, all the animals in that country followed the timberline. I went there early one morning and in less than an hour I had my moose. I dressed the meat and carried it to the cabin. Hung from the meat rack I had made and with a stretched canvas cover about it to stave off rain and snow, it would keep well.

There was plenty for me to do. I brought the hide into camp, and that had to be fleshed and have the hair removed. It would eventually make many feet of rawhide for snowshoes and a dozen other uses. I trapped the river for mink. They were so plentiful I took almost a hundred and fifty in ten days. Every night I worked for hours, fleshing the hides and getting them on the stretcher boards I had made. I knew I had taken enough mink, for I didn't want to deplete them too far, so for the next two months I trapped marten and did well. As February came, time began to pass slowly and I decided to see what the lower river looked like. I packed a few supplies and set out for Harry's cabin at the mouth of Rat Creek. In four hours I had traveled about fifteen miles and I could see the cabin across the frozen river. I hadn't forgotten about my well-packed trail on the river and the ten feet of it that had dropped away behind me. I cut a long birch pole and made the crossing, the pole insurance against going completely under the water if I should break through the snow-covered ice.

I spent the night in Harry's cabin. I had seen plenty of mink signs and intended next fall to extend my trap line down this way. Rat Lake was five miles up Rat Creek and the next morning I went to the cabin there. I shoveled snow away from the door, using one of my snowshoes, and finally got it open.

John's bedroll was lying on the floor. It looked like a short, frozen log. I guessed he had crossed the Tikchik River, probably using a dry log for a float, and everything had been soaked. There was plenty of stove wood in the cabin and more outside, but he hadn't stopped to dry anything out. If he was still living, he was having a rough time. He could never have made it to the Mulchatna. There were too many creeks, too many small rivers and swamps, too much of everything for John.

I didn't stay long. Late that afternoon I was back at my own cabin.

That spring Matt was early. On the first day of March I heard the sound of a plane in the distance. The sound got closer and soon I could see the distinctive look of Matt's biplane, the only one of its kind in Bristol Bay.

He set his plane down on its skis and taxied up to the end of the trail. I was there to meet him when he climbed down and I was glad to see him, but before I could open my mouth he gave me the news.

"Fred, they found your partner."

It didn't come as a surprise but I was still shocked.

"Come on up to the cabin. We'll have some coffee and you can tell me about John."

"Well, Albert Ball was flying up the Wood River Lakes. He saw a man floundering along through deep snow and landed. It was John and he was burned black from frost.

Albert put him in his plane and flew him into Dillingham. All he had with him were the ragged clothes on his back."

"What have they done with him?"

"He was found three weeks ago. They kept him in the hospital two weeks and then flew him out to Seattle. He's in a mental institution."

It seemed this country did strange things to a man. For the first time I wondered if the loneliness, the immensity, would ever get to me like that. The flying time to Dillingham seemed short. I had a lot to think about.

6 / 1939

DILLINGHAM NEVER SEEMED TO CHANGE. Breakup on the rivers signaled the first arrival of the men who lived on them. The fishing season would come and go. Then it was time for all of the trappers to start the long journey back to their winter homes. Some of them worked their way up the rivers as much as a hundred and fifty miles. The rivers were never straight; they curved and bent back and forth, and this added to the miles the men had to travel.

This spring, 1939, the fishing season got off to a late start.

All of the local fishermen had asked for twenty-five cents for each salmon, an increase of nine cents a fish. The Alaskan salmon industry refused, and we sat on the beach. The outside fishermen refused to back us up and we watched as they put out to sea in their sailboats.

That night three fishing boats, tied up at the cannery dock, had the bottoms blown out of them. Across the river at the Libby cannery, the same thing happened. It almost looked as though someone had dropped a stick of dynamite into the bottom of each boat. The next day, after a hurried consultation, the canneries decided twenty-five cents wasn't too much to pay for a salmon. The increase in price, the first in years, made a big difference to the fishermen's payday.

Every fall, when I got my supplies together, I tried to remember anything I might have needed the year before and didn't have. There were miles of open tundra north of my cabin and from the top of the hill, above the lake, I could see large clearings in the timber. In both places I had seen the movement of many animals I hadn't been able to identify. This year I bought a pair of binoculars to take with me. This was going to be my fifth year in the Tikchiks and surely this time I'd have nothing to worry about except myself. I rather liked the idea of giving that country a try with nobody there but me.

In the middle of August Matt and I loaded his plane and left Dillingham. We set down on the lake and unloaded and Matt walked with me to the cabin. Both windows were smashed out and there was a huge hole in one corner of the roof. A grizzly had been there and he'd left his mark.

"Matt, will you be coming back this way any time soon?"

"In about five days. I've got a trip to Aniak."

"Pick up plenty of panes of glass, would you, and drop them off on your way through?"

He helped me get the roof back in shape. It was a matter of laying the split roof logs back where they belonged and covering them with plenty of moss and sod. After he left, I looked around and realized I had been lucky. The stove hadn't been touched. It seemed the windows and the roof had been the main targets.

I spent the next five days waiting for Matt and building a cache. A cache is simply a small five-by-five cabin. The trick is where you put it. First, you place the lower ends of four stout logs in the ground to a depth of three feet, leaving about fifteen feet above ground. Then you build the cache on top of these upright logs. Lengths of stove pipe fitted round the logs stop mice, squirrels or wolverine from getting up into the cache. Grizzlies can't climb, so I had no worry about them. From this time on, when I left in the spring, everything of value in my cabin, including the windowpanes, was stored there.

I had time on my hands, waiting for Matt, but I used it to advantage. I put up enough stove wood to last through the winter and I girdled ten good-sized trees. To girdle a tree you simply cut off the bark in a six-inch circle round the base of the trunk. This prevents any more sap from rising up. Next fall, those ten trees would be dry and ready to use for more stove wood.

In a week, Matt was back with my window glass. After his usual cup of coffee, he said he'd see me in the spring and he left.

I hadn't seen much of the country to the west of me and this seemed like a good time to look around. I followed the timberline most of the time and by midafternoon I had covered maybe twelve miles or so. Down in a small draw, I saw what was left of a cabin and went to take a look. The size, about five by seven feet, told me it had been an outcamp for some trapper. At one time it had been a sturdy little cabin; now it was sagging and ready to fall, the doorway no more than a crawl space. Inside, a small rusty frying pan was lying on the dirt floor and I found loading tools for a .45–70 rifle. Things fell into place now. The man who had built and used this outcamp was the same man who had built the cabin I was living in. He was on the trail somewhere and he wouldn't be coming back. Perhaps this was another score to mark up for a grizzly.

I traveled until evening and made camp on the slope of a timbered hill. My camp was a piece of light canvas hung between two trees, with the lower corners pegged to the ground. From there I could see the fourth and fifth Tikchik lakes. It was a wild and wonderful land and I had the odd feeling that it was all mine. Maybe it was, for in all the years I lived in that country, no one else ever came.

The next morning I took a different route back to my cabin. I was traveling along a ridge, reveling in the knowledge that I was the only man who had ever walked this trail. The thought was still in my mind when ahead of me I saw an old tobacco can on the top of a spruce tree, twenty feet high.

I cut the tree down and looked the can over. It was faded to a pale gray color but on the front I could read the dim letters, Prince Albert. The old trapper had left me a reminder, telling me he was here before I was. He must have placed the can there when the tree was no more than six feet high.

❉ ❉ ❉

I knew I was in grizzly country, but all of them were down on the river and creeks now, feeding on the salmon that had come to spawn and die. I was in high timber, with a sense of freedom from any danger of bears. I arrived home that evening.

The next morning I thought I might as well start laying out mink traps and wiring them fast where my sets would be, and soon after first light I started doing just that.

If a man says he knows everything about grizzly bears he's simply dead wrong, for no man does; we know they're unpredictable, but sometimes they can be more than that. Still, what happened was really my fault. I should have known enough to keep away from the river at that time of year. I was on the trail that followed the Tikchik and as I made the turn around a bend I was facing a grizzly not forty feet ahead of me. A roar of rage was followed by a deliberate movement toward me, his jaws opened wide, the lips curled back. He had heard and smelled me and he had waited. His slow pace made him an easy target and I put a bullet square in his chest, but still he came forward. A second bullet entered his chest. I knew he was damaged, he had to be mortally hurt, but he didn't go down.

The impossible happened then. He rose to his hind feet. He towered three feet above me. From ten feet away I fired a third shot; the impact at that distance must have been terrific. It had no more effect than if I had held my hand up and said, "Stop." His eyes were fixed and staring straight above me. I stepped a short distance off the trail and watched him. He moved ahead, step by slow step. When at last he fell forward, his body covered the place where I had been.

He had been dead for several seconds but he had moved ahead, erect on his hind feet, at least ten feet. His body had been dead but his brain simply didn't know it. The palm of my hand covered the place where the three shots had gone in. I don't have to say I waited to work the river until later that fall. I waited until the middle of November, when I knew the river was clear of grizzlies.

One morning I approached a mink set that I had made under the branches of a spruce tree. I bent down to take a look at it and a snarling mouth, full of long sharp teeth, leapt out from under the branches at the same time. It was a wolverine and he didn't miss me by very much.

A wolverine looks like a small bear. In weight, they will run from twenty to forty pounds of solid bone and muscle and in a trap they have no thought except to tear up everything they can reach. They are black in color and have a long bushy tail, a foot long. There is always a cream-colored diamond shape on their backs. This may be eighteen inches in length and ten inches wide and the center of it is black too. Unlike most fur, wolverine won't collect frost and for this reason it is prized for use as parka hoods. It is a beautiful fur.

This wolverine had huge paws, tipped with razor-sharp claws. My trap was small—it was meant for mink—but it was wired to a willow that had plenty of spring in it. He had been caught by two front toes and hadn't been there long. Because I thought there would be no bears around, I carried no rifle but I had a small camp axe in my pack. I tried to strike his head, but he was fast. He backed under the branches and when he thought I was close enough, out he came, claws reaching and mouth wide open.

I cut down a slender birch pole and sharpened the end of it. He made a try for me and I rammed the pole into the earth, pulling it down hard across his back to hold him, and with the head of my axe, I hammered on his head. He didn't quit until I had battered in his skull.

Once a wolverine locates a trapline you must either trap him or give up the line. They won't miss a set and you'll be left with maybe a mink tail or part of a fox skin. Many trappers find them difficult to take but if you're familiar with the habits of any animal, it can be trapped. I have heard tales that a wolverine is clever enough to turn a trap over and leave it upside down. That is true, in a way. Catching that one in a mink set had been an accident on his part. I have watched a wolverine approach a set. About three feet from the trap, he methodically scratched up every inch of snow or earth. Eventually, his claws hooked the chain and the trap was pulled out of place—once in a while, it will land upside down, still set. I waited until he finished his approach, and then I shot him.

Greed is their downfall. When I realized one of them was working my trapline over, I would take a good-sized piece of any kind of meat, and locate two or three small trees close together and near my trail. The trees need to be just inches apart, so they can be easily climbed. I would wire the meat in place as high as I could reach and then set three number four traps beneath the bait, making no attempt to cover them. The wolverine will approach the set, and carefully avoiding the traps, he will climb the trees and tear the meat loose. As he backs down the trees with his prize, he is thinking only of the juicy meat in his jaws. He has forgotten the traps. He will step in at least two of them. You will hear him long before you reach the set. Wolverine have a screaming roar that can be heard for a long way. As you approach the set, he will not try to escape. His only desire is to have you in his teeth and claws. Everything within his reach will already be chewed or torn down.

Wolverine will avoid a cabin but there was one time that a wolverine visited mine, when I was gone for the day. Cans of fruit had been bitten into. Some of my dishes were smashed and several of the pots and pans were punched full of holes by his teeth. Bags of flour and sugar were torn open and some strewn over the floor. You could feel the hate he'd left behind. Only a grizzly can cause more damage.

A wolverine bears its young in February, and at that time they can be even more dangerous and may attack unprovoked. On two occasions I heard one come charging through the brush, crying its high-pitched scream. They are difficult, then, to hit with a rifle: they come in a weaving, bobbing charge. However, a shot fired will turn them.

I trapped mink for two weeks and quit. I had enough and that river was my fur farm. I wanted good trapping next year and for all the years I might live in that country. The river began to fill with frozen slush. This settles to the bottom and keeps building up. Before long, the water is over the banks and spreading out through the brush; anything you have left on your trapline is lost to the river. It was an added incentive for me to pull my traps.

This was my fourth winter in the Tikchiks and for the first time things had gone well with me. I was never lonely. I was always glad to get away from town and the crowd of people. Whenever Matt left me in the fall, it was as though a line was drawn between me and the rest of the world. Sometimes I wondered if that was a good thing. When you are alone that way, you do a tremendous amount of thinking. You have a tendency to form your own opinion about everything, perhaps too much so. The only escape for me was reading. Every fall I brought in more books, and turning to them for a direction other than my own, I was all right.

My binoculars were a wonderful thing. They opened up a new world for me. The hill rising from the lake shore was fairly long and high. There were several deep gullies coursing down the side of it, and sometimes one of them was a resting place for a grizzly. I had made a habit of always stopping by the small gut of water that joined the two lakes together and from there I could look the hill over carefully. One day as I sat there I saw a fox, lying by the small mound of earth that marked his den. This was a new home for him, for I knew I had passed by that spot many times and seen nothing. I watched for some time and finally he rose to his feet. As he stood there I could see a bare spot on his hip, and I knew it had been caused by an injury. A wolverine was the only thing I could think of that might have done it. I stood up, and he either saw me or smelled me, for he turned and disappeared inside his den.

There were always plenty of spruce grouse around and I shot one the next day. The feathers came off with the skin and I walked with the meat up the hill to the den, placing it just outside. Back at the small gut of water I sat down and watched. First his head appeared and after a careful scrutiny he emerged a bit more, enough to reach the meat with his mouth. He took it and dropped back into his home.

I had about a month with nothing much to do and I made that fox my project. Every day I took a piece of grouse meat and as I walked past his home, I dropped it there. I knew he was aware of every move I made. The day came when I walked up the hill and his head was outside. I dropped the meat and kept on going. The time finally came when I walked up the hill and he was standing there, waiting for me, watchful but unafraid. I dropped the meat and walked back down the hill. In time I could approach him and toss the meat and stand there while he picked it up and retreated down into his den. Never once would he take a step toward me, though. After I got my moose later that fall, I gave him a small piece every day. Stronger and fitter, he would stand and eat it while I watched, but he would never let me put my hand on him.

In late fall, the hill was covered with frozen blueberries. These are very short plants, the berries barely showing above the moss. When snow covered the ground, they provided food for the many mice that were there. This hill was the fox's winter hunting ground. I watched with my binoculars as he traveled in a direct line, walking slowly and carefully, his tail erect. I could see him cringe when one of his feet broke through the snow. Then he stopped, his tail straightened out and he made a leap of at least six feet. He went through the air like an arrow to its mark. When he landed, his forepaws and muzzle were bunched together as they drove into the snow, when he raised his head he had a mouse in his mouth. His acute sense of smell had enabled him to pinpoint its location to the very inch. It was a lesson to me in the way animals have developed their senses in the never-ending quest for survival.

❈ ❈ ❈

My winters didn't change very much. First it was fall, then winter came. As usual, December was the cold month. The day before Christmas I knew there was something I wanted to do on Christmas morning. There would be no real Christmas for me, but I could do this. At five o'clock I got into my warmest clothing. It wasn't daybreak yet but the sky had lightened a little. I went outside and strapped on my snowshoes. It wasn't far to the top of the hill by the lake but the frigid cold made me hustle, and it didn't take me long to get there. There wasn't a star left in the sky above but off in the east I saw what I had come for. It was the morning star. It was big and beautiful and had a shining glory all its own. This was the star in the east, the star the wise men had followed.

I always thought of my family at Christmas time and I did now. I thought of my mother and dad, my brother and my sisters. They were far away but I knew they would be thinking of me, too.

I turned away and walked down the hill, back to the cabin. The warmth inside felt good. I don't know why I had never brought a radio in with me. Next fall I surely would, for days like this were a little lonely.

That night I stepped outside and saw the Northern Lights—not the usual display in the sky: these were all around the cabin and through the trees, wavering bands of brilliant blue and scarlet, shining streamers of golden light, close to the surface of the snow and as far in the sky as I could see. I walked through the trees and the backs of my hands and my face had a prickly feeling. I was in a world of make-believe. I stopped and turned. I could see the small flicker of my lamp in the cabin window and it seemed to tell me to come back. Sometimes your mind will grasp at a random fantasy. I never again, in all the years I lived in that country, saw a display as beautiful as I did that night. The colors moved through the trees with a sound so hushed it was like softly moving silk.

February is always a rough, blustery month. One day I didn't leave the cabin, for the weather was such that I could barely see the lake shore from my window. Clouds of snow were blowing across the ice.

I was sitting at the table, looking out at the storm, and I saw the plane as it set down on the snow at the edge of the lake. There was no sound of a plane, it was simply there, and its door opened. I saw the man who climbed out and I knew him. It was Heine Hildebrandt and the plane belonged to Orville Braswell; I recognized it. I couldn't believe a plane could fly in that weather, much less find my small lake. I put my coat on and went out, hurrying down the trail, but before I got to the lake shore I could see the plane wasn't there. I walked to where it had landed. There wasn't a sign on the snow. No ski marks, no footprints where the man had walked, there was nothing at all.

I walked back to the cabin and sat down and gave a lot of thought to what I had seen. Nothing made any sense. That evening, just at dusk, I picked up the five-gallon kerosene can I had made into a pail and walked the short distance to the open creek where I got my water. I had filled the can and was halfway back to the cabin, when I heard the voices: "It's down there. It's right down there."

I set the can down and shouted, "I'll be right up." The voices had come from the timberline and I knew there were people there, looking for my cabin. I went inside and grabbed the flashlight, came out and slipped into my snow-shoes. I hurried up the timbered slope and in a very short time was out in the open. I called but there was no answer. I walked out on the open tundra for at least two hundred yards, looking for the marks of a dog sled; I knew there had to be something. There was no sign that anyone had been there.

For the second time that day I went back to the cabin and began to wonder if perhaps there was something wrong with me. I had seen a plane that wasn't there and now I had just heard, very plainly, spoken words and yet no one had been there. After a while, I simply refused to think about it.

Matt stopped off to see me in early March. He was on his way back from the head of the Stony River and he had swung over my way to visit. I was always glad to see him. We had coffee and talked and he told me the news.

"Fred, you left town too early last fall to hear what's happening. Germany and Russia invaded Poland, then France and Great Britain declared war on Germany. Half of Europe is at war."

"It's only been about twenty years since the last big one. I hope we don't get into it."

During the winter I'd had a little pain in my right side once in a while, and I thought I might have a touch of appendicitis. That, and most of all Matt's news of war, made me want to get back to the coast. I made up my mind.

"Matt, if you'll give me a hand, I'll go out with you now."

It didn't take us long to get ready to leave and when we landed in Dillingham, Matt's pickup was there. We loaded my fur and the few things I had brought out with me and he drove me to the trading store.

Tubby was surprised to see me. There was no one in town yet, he said, just the few who had wintered there. There was a man I wanted to see, though, and I went to his cabin. I had known Orville Braswell since I had been in Dillingham.

"Orville, where were you in February, about the tenth of the month?"

"I was trapping beaver up on the Mulchatna. I stayed there the second and third weeks of February."

"You had Heine Hildebrandt with you."

Orville gave me a long look. "How would you know that? You just got in town."

"I saw your plane setting down on the edge of the little lake where I live. I saw Heine climb out and walk a few steps in the snow. My cabin isn't over a hundred yards from where you were. When I got out of the cabin and started down the trail, there was nothing there. No plane and no footprints in the snow."

"I've never been where you live, Fred, but I know the Mulchatna is at least two hundred miles east of there."

"There was a blizzard that day and even if you had known where I live, you couldn't have been flying. I was sitting at the table, looking out the window. There was nothing there and then I saw the plane and I saw Heine. It was only a few seconds before I was out the cabin door, and then you weren't there."

I left Orville's cabin with a strange feeling. He'd confirmed that Heine had been with him in February, even that they'd been flying that month, but nothing else made sense.

❋ ❋ ❋

Tubby was a good friend and if I needed his pickup, it was mine. I drove to the hospital run by the Bureau of Indian Affairs. There was just the one doctor and he took care of everything, from colds and fever to broken bones and surgery.

Dr. Salazar poked and prodded and sat back in his chair.

"You've got a touch of appendicitis. You could probably get by for a long time but if I was a trapper and stayed up in the woods the best part of the year, the way you do, I'd have that appendix out. Can you come back in the morning?"

"I'll be here."

There were four cars in town. Tubby and Matt each had a pickup, the school teacher had a small car and Jessie Pelagio had a taxi. Next morning, Jessie drove me to the hospital. I got into a shower and scrubbed down and in no time at all I was on my back on the operating table.

"Fred, have you ever had a spinal injection?"

"All I've ever had is a vaccination."

"We'll try a spinal."

"I'd like to be able to watch you work, Doc. Could you have some pillows put under my shoulders?"

"Sure, if you want to see how this is done, we'll prop you up."

They had me roll over on my stomach; his nurse had the syringe in her hand.

"Doctor, his back muscles almost cover his spine. I'm having a job finding a place for the needle."

"Yeah, Fred does a lot of backpacking. You can find a way through."

I felt just a slight pinprick in my back. "There, I think I have it."

They rolled me over on my back again and the nurse standing behind me placed two or three pillows under my head and shoulders. Dr. Salazar marked the spot for the incision and the nurse painted the area with some antiseptic. With his scalpel, the doctor traced a small line.

"Can you feel that?"

"Yes, I can feel it."

"We'll wait a few seconds. Fred, I'm not going to cut across any muscles, I'm going to split each one as we go in."

He made his first incision and it felt as though he had lighted a fire on my stomach. He kept up a running commentary.

"There's no fat in here, Fred, it's going to make things a lot easier."

I think I read somewhere that pain has a peak. Beyond that, it can't get any worse. I knew they were using red-hot tongs and they were pulling out all my insides.

"Fred, this is a dandy. I think it's the longest appendix I've ever seen. No wonder your side hurt." He held it up for me to see and dropped it into a jar of alcohol.

I had lost all interest in watching him work. I was staring at the ceiling, trying to hang on. I hadn't seen the nurse while he worked. She was standing by my head and I felt her hands as she placed them either side of my face.

"Doctor, this is no time to be teaching someone how to tie knots."

"Give him some ether."

"Doc, I don't want ether. It'll make me sick."

"Get this man closed up."

In not more than a half minute the incision was sewn up and I felt better. I'm not sure what he called the narrow table with wheels that always seem to wobble. Whatever it was, he told the nurse at my head to have them bring it in and take me to my room.

I swung my legs over the edge of the operating table and stood up.

"Don't bother, I can walk."

I left then and walked down the corridor to my room and was sitting on the edge of my bed when Salazar followed me in. I suppose the fact that I could walk told him the anesthetic hadn't had its effect.

"Fred, why in the world didn't you tell me that the spinal didn't work?"

"I thought maybe it was supposed to feel that way. I'm glad it's over, though."

"Once in a while we find someone that a spinal doesn't work on. You're one of them. You're going to have a splitting headache. I'll send your nurse in with some pills."

She came with the pills and a glass of water and put them on the small table by my bed.

"You're a stubborn man."

She couldn't weigh over ninety pounds soaking wet and she was a pretty thing.

"Are you going to be my nurse?"

"Yes, I am. I'm Ann Peterson. Now take these pills." I knew by her voice that she was the nurse who had been standing by my head. There wasn't a trace of a smile on her face, and there should have been. The pills were in a small plastic cup. I swallowed them and took a sip of water.

"You try to get some rest. If you need me, press the buzzer." She turned away and left the room.

I wondered about her. She had shown concern when I was on that operating table. She wasn't as remote and cold as she pretended to be.

One of the pills she had given me wasn't for a headache and before I knew it I was sound asleep. Three more days went by this way. She would bring my meals, and after a while she would come back and pick up the tray. The fourth evening when she came to take my tray, I knew I had to act. There was something about her that made me want to know her.

"Ann, I'll be leaving in the morning. Do you think you'd like to come and sit with me a little while tonight? There's a radio here. We can listen to that and perhaps we can talk."

She looked at me and it seemed a long time before she nodded her head.

"I might be a little late. There are things I have to do, but I'll be here."

7 / *Ann*

It was ten o'clock that night when she came and sat by my bed. The music from the radio was soft and low.

"Ann, you've never told me anything about yourself. I don't know how old you are. I don't even know where you come from."

She sat silent for a little time before she answered.

"I'm nineteen years old. I was born on St. Paul Island in the Pribilofs. It's out in the Bering Sea, two hundred and fifty miles from the Aleutian Chain.

"My father was from Sweden. He worked on St. Paul for the government, helping the people who lived there, people who looked after the fur seal herds. The seal come there to have their young and breed again.

"My father's name was Steve Peterson. He married a girl named Martha Shabiloff. She was Aleut and Russian. When I was one year old my father died of pneumonia. My grandfather operated a herring saltery at Unalaska, in the Aleutian Islands, and my mother took me there and we lived with him.

"When I was five years old I saw my mother fall to the ground in our yard. I ran to her and tried to make her get up. I didn't understand but she had died from a heart attack. I stayed with my grandfather until he died. I was ten years old then. I stayed with one family, then another and another. If someone had work to be done, they came and took me. Sometimes I think I was bought and sold."

She dragged driftwood from the beach to the families she lived with. When she was twelve years old, she was raped. Those were some of the things she told me.

There were silent tears on her face. I took her hand and she came to me and I held her in my arms the way I would a child. I smoothed away the tears and I could feel her relax in my arms. It was then I knew I loved her.

"When I was fourteen, a woman came to Unalaska to teach. She found me and sent me here. There was an Indian Affairs School at Eklutna, not far from Anchorage, and Salazar had me go there to study. When I was seventeen I came back. I've been a student nurse for two years."

She was quiet now and I held her close.

"Ann, things are going to be different, you'll see. If you let me, I'll pick you up some evening and we can go into town, get to know each other."

"Yes," she said. "I'd like to go with you."

I stayed awake quite a while after she left me. I thought how fine it would be to have someone like her, but I couldn't see how any girl would want to live the way I did.

The next morning she brought my breakfast.

"Well, I'm leaving this morning. But I'm coming back tomorrow night. I'm going to take you into town."

She nodded and I think there was a trace of a smile on her face. "I'll be ready."

I was there by seven o'clock and Ann had been waiting, for she was out of the door and over to the pickup almost as soon as it stopped. She was radiant and beautiful. I opened the door and she was sitting beside me.

At that time the only shows we had in town were cowboy movies. Even so, everyone liked them, for we were seeing a different world. No one seemed to mind the blue haze of tobacco smoke in the air; this was a time for enjoyment. When the show was over we had a meal in the restaurant, and when we arrived back at the hospital I got out with her.

"When do you get a day off?"

"Next Thursday."

"I'll be out to get you. We'll spend the day together." She gave a little quick nod. I put my arms round her and hugged her for a moment. I watched her as she walked up the steps; before she opened the door and went inside, she turned and waved.

Thursday was three more days and every day I gave a lot of thought to Ann. I wasn't sure how to go about something like this.

I was at the hospital by nine o'clock Thursday morning. We drove down the dirt road toward town and when we came to the Wood River turnoff, I followed it. There was a cannery on the bank and we stopped there. It was still March and the fishing season was three months away so the cannery was deserted. We walked out onto the dock. The morning was sunny and warm and we sat down on some timber that was lying there. The flood tide came up the river this far and the salt water had eaten away at the ice. Water was surging out of the open places, it was flowing over the frozen surface, and in a few more days this part of the river would be free. Far to the north I could see the tops of a mountain range. They marked the Tikchik lakes and I lived thirty miles north of there.

"Ann, do you know how I live?" I turned to her then, expecting to have to tell her, but her answer was ready, quiet and calm.

"Yes, I do. You go out in a sailboat and fish for salmon one month every summer. Every fall, you fly into the

Tikchiks, where the big lakes are. You stay in there at least nine months."

"Ann, will you marry me and go to that big lake country with me?"

"Fred, I will. I'll marry you and I'll go wherever you go."

That was what she said. When I took her in my arms I felt like a king. Her lips were soft and yielding.

"I'll never make you sorry, Ann."

We drove into town and I left her at my cabin. I walked down to the Scandinavian Cannery store. It was the only place I could hope to find a ring. I found one and it cost me two and a half dollars. I went back for Ann and we walked to the commissioner's office. He was a new one and I didn't know him very well.

He asked us both our names and wrote them down.

"Do you, Ann Peterson, take this man to be your lawful wedded husband?"

"I do."

"Do you, Fred Hatfield, take this woman to be your lawful wedded wife?"

"I do."

"By the authority vested in me by my commission, I pronounce you man and wife."

I turned to Ann. I could see joy, hope and happiness. It was all there and I took her in my arms and held her very close.

I hadn't planned to fish that summer—the doctor had told me I'd probably pull some stitches. That was fine with me, for I wanted to have the summer with Ann.

She changed almost overnight from a lonely girl into a serene woman. For the first time she had someone she could confide in, she could talk to about her hopes and dreams. She made our cabin into a home and she made me a happy man.

She brought something every day, some little thing she wanted to take with her when the time came for us to leave.

❄ ❄ ❄

Peetla was an old Eskimo from the village of Stuyahok, far up the Nushagak river. He didn't work anymore but he came down the river in the spring, with his people. If the weather was good he spent his time sitting on a bench in front of the trading store. We were friends and when I had the time I would sit with him, for there were many things he would tell me.

One day I saw Peetla in his favorite place. I went over and sat down beside him and he finally turned to me.

"You Tikchik man."

I nodded in agreement.

"You kill many bears in Tikchiks?"

"Only when I have to."

"I tell you best way. You wait, wait, till plenty close. Maybe close so you smell him. Maybe five, six feet. Point gun at his mouth. When you pull trigger, bear is dead. Back of head gone. Or maybe point under chin. Same thing."

Peetla looked out over the bay. I knew he had something more to tell me but I would have to wait until he was ready. I knew he was telling me the truth, for the grizzly that had jumped me above Jake Savolly's cabin had been that close.

Before the native people had access to rifles, a spear was their only weapon. They never hunted alone. Three of them together, all armed with stout spears pointed with bone or ivory, and razor sharp, made determined adversaries even against a savage grizzly. They used their spears the same way Peetla had told me to use my rifle.

At close quarters a grizzly is standing. He is roaring in rage and his mouth is opened wide. A spear driven deep down his throat or, as Peetla had said, "maybe under chin," resulted in a very sick grizzly, one that would die quickly. Eventually the people obtained rifles. The first was the big .45–70 Winchester. Armed with that, they could see no reason to change their method of defense, for the big rifle worked much better than their spears and in any case a rifle was something new to them and they were not good shots with it. The .45–70 was eventually replaced by the .30–06, but they used it in the same way on a grizzly.

Peetla was still looking out over the bay.

"Tikchiks bad place for you. You got woman now. Tikchiks no good."

I waited. I knew he wasn't finished. Then he turned to me.

"Maybe you see things in Tikchiks? Maybe you hear things?"

He had me really interested now, for I hadn't forgotten the plane or the voices I had heard.

Peetla looked at me, his gaze intent. When he spoke again his voice was deliberate.

"But then you see no one and nothing there?"

"That's right."

He nodded. "Long time ago, long before me, many people live there. Big village on first lake. Many, many people. 'Most every day, someone see something, maybe they hear something. Nothing there. They tell about this and my people laugh. The old people don't laugh. They tell how many gods live there. This is the place of the Great Spirit. My people laugh some more.

"One time, a bad thing happen. All my people die. Not many left. In spring, when the ice go away, they get in their boats and they come down the rivers. They come to the Nushagak. No one ever go back again. Fred, maybe one day a bad thing happen to you. Tikchiks, place where many gods live. You come to my village. Plenty fur, many friends."

Peetla was a kind, fine old man and he believed every

word he told me. In his mind, he was right. I didn't want to
hurt his feelings so I said I would give it a lot of thought.

❋ ❋ ❋

The year I had lived at Togiak Lake I had seen a high peak
just north of the upper lake. On the map it was named
Mount Waskey.

In 1906 the United States decided it was time that the
Territory of Alaska had a delegate to represent it in Washing-
ton. Nome was the largest town in Alaska at that time and
the election was held there. Frank Waskey and Judge Wick-
ersham were the two men running and the votes came out
exactly even. A coin was tossed and when it landed Frank
Waskey was the first elected Alaska delegate to the House of
Representatives.

Frank Waskey lived in Dillingham now. We were friends
and I knew he was the most well-informed man in Alaska on
native history and culture. He had traveled all over, looking
and digging for artifacts. Most of the things he found he
donated to the University of Alaska. The other things he
found were friends. In the winter months he spent a good
part of his time flying up the rivers, wherever there were
trappers. He bought all of their wolverine skins and resold
them at the settlements on the Yukon River. He paid fifty
dollars for each skin and that was a good price, much more
than the fur buyers would pay.

I needed to talk to Frank and I went to his cabin. I told
him Peetla's story and I told him of the plane I had seen and
the voices I had heard.

"Fred, you've handed me a difficult problem. I know I
don't have the exact answer but I think I'm close to it. I knew
Harry Stevens when he trapped the Tikchiks. Now, he was a
sane man and yet two different years he heard voices and
saw things that simply weren't there. Peetla's people have
known of these things since they first went into that country,

probably hundreds of years ago. In fact his people died from a smallpox epidemic but to them, they were being punished by the gods for being in there.

"I've given a lot of thought to that country. It's the combination of positions that matters, I think, the shape and direction of the mountain ranges, the long chain of big lakes, perhaps the huge expanse of open tundra north of there, too. Who knows? Maybe what you see is a refracted image of what's too far off to be seen in reality. But I do know one thing. That area is a focal point for objects and sounds. It's as though somewhere there's a huge projector, with sound, focused on that area. That's a poor way to say it, for the plane you saw had no sound and the voices you heard weren't produced by anyone you could see. I can't really tell you any more. There must be other places on this earth that are the same way, but I've never heard of them."

"I can't say it ever really bothers me, Frank. I wondered about it for a time but I knew there was an answer of some kind. I was glad to hear Peetla's story and I'm glad to hear yours. I live in there and I wouldn't like to think I was the only man who ever experienced something like that. It's a beautiful country and I like your theory. I don't mind living in a focal point."

"If you see anything else or hear something else, let me know about it. I'm going to think about it some more and I probably will for a long time. I don't think we'll ever know the real answer, Fred."

❊ ❊ ❊

It was June 5 and the Trappers' Ball was to be held that night. Ann and I were going and I knew she would have the surprise of her life, for she had never seen anything like this. The place was crowded. I think everyone who could walk was there. Many of the people had Swedish ancestry and the Swedish polka seemed to be the favorite dance, lusty and vigorous. The walls echoed stamping feet and the music from Red's piano.

I wasn't an expert dancer and I soon lost Ann. I'd find myself going the wrong way but on that crowded floor it wasn't hard to do. It didn't seem to matter at all, for there was always some lady who found herself in the same fix I was and we'd go stamping down the floor together. No one seemed to have the same partner very long, and once in a while I'd find Ann.

Shortly after midnight the ball was over and Ann and I walked home.

"Honey, was it fun?"

"I didn't think anyone could ever have fun like that. Everyone was so friendly and happy."

"In the fall they have the Fishermen's Ball, but I've always left town before that. People here don't have many chances for a good time, so they sure make the most of it."

❇   ❇   ❇

In the latter part of July Ann and I started writing down our list of supplies. She put down every spice she could think of and every cooking extract. I doubled the amount of some things I had been taking with me every fall and bought a shortwave RCA radio. It was powered by a big drycell battery and I took an extra one of those, too. This year I took a roll of canvas and two gallons of paint, for I wanted to have a good roof on our cabin. I thought some more and decided to buy an eight-by-ten tent and another Yukon stove. There was always a chance that fire would take our cabin, and if so, these would give us shelter and warmth. I had Ann now and I took every precaution for her safety.

It was a fair day in early August when we left town. We passed over the Wood River lakes and crossed a small range of mountains. It was all familiar to me but for Ann it was a new world. We passed over the first of the Tikchik lakes, then we were in beautiful country. Far to the north we could see a high mountain range. West of us were more rugged mountains, some of the peaks buried in the sky. East of the Tikchik Valley there were endless miles of swamp and tundra, small ranges of hills and then the Nushagak River, then more miles and then the Mulchatna.

Ahead of us in the distance I could see where our home was. It had been a lonely place, just a little lake with no name, so I had given it one. The miles of spruce trees stopped there so I named it Spruce Lake. A name pegged it down in the wilderness, gave me some kind of bearing, some sense of place.

Matt, as he always did, circled low over the hill by the lake. We were about twelve feet in the air. As he made his approach turn and got ready to set down on the water, a huge grizzly suddenly stood on his hind legs and reached for the floats. Matt pulled back hard and we rose up sharply. He turned to me and shook his head and I looked at Ann. Her face was frozen in disbelief. Matt made another circle and we landed. Ann climbed out of the plane and stood anxiously on the shore while we unloaded our supplies.

"Fred, does that bear live here?"

"Ann, honey, I think that bear is three miles from here now and still going. He thought the biggest bird in the world was after him."

I didn't tell her this was grizzly country. I didn't think it was the right moment.

For the first time, Matt was going to have to make two trips; his old Waco biplane just wasn't big enough to bring in all we needed. He said he'd be back in about three hours and left. That way he could be in and out again well before dark.

I got both our packboards out and my rifle. We loaded up with what we could carry and went up the narrow trail to the cabin. It wasn't very far and when we got there Ann didn't seem to mind the hard-packed dirt floor, she didn't mind the bed that was just a six-foot width of springy poles, but when she saw the ragged hole in the roof, a hole so big you could drive a small truck through it, she turned to me.

"Did that bear do that?"

"Well, maybe not that bear but some bear did, maybe two or three of them. We'll have it fixed in no time."

First we had to get our goods close to the cabin. We had just about finished when we heard the hum of Matt's plane in the distance.

I told him the bears had ruined my cabin roof again and he insisted on giving me a hand to get things in shape.

"Well, back in the middle of April, folks."

When a plane sets you down in the wilderness some-where and then leaves, you always watch it. You watch it in the sky until it isn't there any more. I broke in on Ann's thoughts.

"Welcome home, honey."

She came to me in a rush, then, and held on. I knew how she felt.

There was plenty to do and most of it, this first night, I wanted done before dark. With my hunting knife, I started cutting the long hay between the trees. I carried a good big pile of it inside the cabin and spread it over the bed poles in a thick layer. I took Ann to the cache and climbed the ladder against the side. Opening the small hinged door, I tossed down two tanned moose hides, blankets and pillows. We carried everything inside the cabin and I nailed one edge of the hides to the log wall. Ann helped me stretch them over the thick hay and I nailed the other sides to the logs on the far edge of our bed. I spread out the blankets and placed the pillows at the head.

Ann reached with a tentative hand and pushed down on the blankets, then she climbed on the bed and stretched out with her head on the pillows. There was a smile on her face.

"I've never had a bed this nice." She was trying hard to make me think things were fine.

I went back to the cache and got the windows and stove. In no time at all the windows were in place and the stove was huffing and puffing.

I went to our pile of supplies and separated it into what would go in the cache and what should come inside with us. Ann got busy putting things away on the shelves. We set our radio on a shelf above the bed and I ran the antenna wire out between logs, a piece of rubber wrapped round it where it went through the wall.

"Honey, I'm going outside to fasten the other end to the top of a pole. I'll walk with it and when the sound is loud and clear, you holler and I'll plant the pole."

I turned the radio on and found a station. Outside I walked around in all directions till I heard Ann yell, then I planted the pole where I was standing. When I got back she was turning the dial and there were stations everywhere, coming in loud and clear. I felt relieved. That radio would be company for Ann when I was away from the cabin.

I still had plenty to do outside. The things that would go in the cache had to be covered with a canvas tarp—there wasn't enough daylight left to put them away now—and I needed enough wood in the cabin to last overnight.

I heard Ann call from the cabin. "Fred. Guess what?"

"What?"

"I've got Quito. Where's that?"

"Quito is in Ecuador and Ecuador is in South America. Are you sure it said Quito?"

"That's what they said."

I went to the cabin.

"Quito has an altitude of almost two miles in the Andes mountains. I guess we don't have any interference in here. I'll bet we can reach 'most anywhere." We did. We got reception at Spruce Lake from all over the world.

Our small lake was alive with northern pike and now I took the fishing rod down there and tied a spinner on the end of the line. The third cast produced a strong yank and I hauled in. It was a big fish. I filleted it on the lake shore and took the boned pieces back to the cabin. Ann had both lamps lit as I came back up the trail. There was a chopping board hanging on a nail on the wall. I took it down and put it on the table with our supper laid on it. Ann rolled it in flour and before long I could smell fish frying and coffee brewing. We were finding our way home.

Next morning I took the roll of heavy canvas I'd brought with us and spread it over the roof. I nailed it fast to the eave logs, and with the two gallons of paint gave it a good thick coat. When I had been alone, the cache had been just a place to put the windows and the stove and if there were a few odds and ends of supplies left, they went there too. With Ann in the cabin it was different. We needed more room, yet we had more things, so the extra stove and the tent went up aloft, and a big roll of extra blankets and a supply of every staple food we had brought in with us. No matter what might happen, Ann and I would survive quite well.

I went up on the hill to see how my friend had made it through the summer. His den was there, but it hadn't been used for some time. I went back down. At the small gut of water where I used to watch him, I noticed a school of small whitefish. I'd tried to catch them before with dry flies and spinners, I'd set out a small meshed gillnet, and nothing had worked. The gut was about three feet wide and six inches deep where it joined our lake with the smaller one and as the fish passed through it I sat down and watched them. They circled the smaller lake, from right to left, and passed in front of me through the little stretch of water and circled our lake, from right to left. Then they passed in front of me again, through the little stretch of water, on their way back. I went to the cabin and got Ann, for I wanted her to take part in a new way to fish.

We placed a line of small stones across the trickle of water at our end, and waited. The whitefish entered the gut and we put a row of stones behind them and scooped them out with our hands. They were just about pan size and they were delicious. After that, every time we thought we'd like whitefish for dinner, that's the way we caught them.

It was fall and the berries were ripe, the hills covered with a shimmer of blue and red; wherever there was an open spot, the blueberries and cranberries grew. One day Ann and I went out on the tundra. There was a small patch there blue with berries. We each had a small pail and were busy picking.

"Fred, look on the top of that hill."

There was a rise at the edge of the flat and three grizzlies were standing there. Two of them stayed where they were but the third one didn't. He came down the slope and stood at the edge of our berry patch. I sat Ann down on a hummock.

"I don't want you to move. No matter what you think might happen, you stay where you are."

I picked a place close to her and sat down myself, slipping a shell into the chamber of my rifle. That gave me five shots.

In the open, a grizzly that wants to look you over will come in a way and stand up. He'll roar and bellow and thump his chest, just to show his authority. Sometimes you're able to move away slowly and be in the clear. Then again, he may drop down and move in closer. He'll stand again and thump his chest, and click his teeth. If he does that he means business and you'll have to kill him.

This bear didn't do any of those things. He started to move across in front of us, then he turned and crossed back the other way, each time getting a little closer.

"Fred, I'm scared."

"No, you're not. You're just not sure what's going to happen. You don't have to worry. He doesn't know I've got a rifle."

He was about a hundred yards away. I would rather he'd been closer, but when a steady menacing growl came from his throat, I knew it was time. At the end of his turn he paused and I fired. I took him just behind the shoulder and I knew I'd hit his heart and lungs. You wouldn't think so. He wheeled and came for us, so fast that when he fell he made a half-turn in the air and landed on his back, his head away from us.

The two grizzlies on the slope were gone and ours wasn't moving. I walked over to him. My bullet had gone in at the right spot. He had been dead before he made his run for us.

We filled our pails with blueberries and went home. We set our pails on the table and Ann sat on the edge of the bed, looking at me.

"That won't happen every time we go somewhere, honey. I've passed by bears when they were picking berries with a packload of meat on my back. They'll look up and then go on as they were, eating berries."

"This one was eating berries." Ann was getting the measure of grizzlies and I was glad she didn't blame me for not outsmarting them every time.

❄ ❄ ❄

In the summer months this lake country seemed to be vacation land for the wolf packs. Food was easy for them to find, but after the first snowfall they left and headed north to where the caribou wintered. I never trapped them, for wolves seemed to me just like beautiful dogs that had never been tamed.

I stepped outside the cabin one evening and I heard a sound in the distance. I heard it again, and it was closer. The wolves were singing and they were coming our way. I went in the cabin and Ann and I put our warm coats on. I took my rifle and flashlight and we walked down to the lake shore and found a good place to sit and wait. It was dark now, and at night, if wolves get the scent of people, they will always come to look things over. Before long, they were all around us.

A wolf starts his song very low. It will keep rising, higher and higher until it is lost in silence. Then another will start and they keep on until they have all had their turn.

"Fred, are wolves as lonely as they sound?"

"I think a wolf is the proudest animal on earth. I can't believe they're lonely. I think they sing a song of life and death. Wolves have to kill to eat and live, but they take only what they need for food."

The wolves' song died away and they drifted off into the night. There were stars overhead now and night sounds all around. Beyond the lake we heard *aaugh! aaugh!* as a bear let us know he was there. Off to the west, in a low willow area, we heard the guttural grunt of a moose. Right in front of us, not twenty feet away, there was a loud splash in the water as a huge pike rose to take something. Night was the time for wild things.

Our radio was a wonderful pastime for us and we enjoyed the evenings. We had lively music from Central and South America and we had programs from the States. There was news of the war in Europe, but that seemed far away.

It was cool enough for meat to keep now and I wanted to get our winter supply ready. Ann had got over her scare from the grizzly in the berry patch but she knew we were in bear country.

"Fred, you be careful."

I kissed her and told her I would and headed for the game trail along the timberline. It was kind of a good feeling to know that someone worried about me. It had been a long time since I'd had anything like that.

I got our meat supply but not just the way I thought I would. I followed the game trail until I reached a slope above the river and saw a cow moose standing at the bottom. I got directly above her and she made no attempt to move. Soon I saw why. One front leg was broken and her side had been raked so badly that her ribs were showing.

I heard grunting and snuffling in the brush behind her. The wind was in my favor so I worked my way down the slope, and passed her. She looked forlorn and lost. I knew what I was going to find. I worked through the brush very slowly and didn't have far to go.

The grizzly was busy ripping and tearing something. I waited for a side shot and picked a spot behind the shoulder, low, and the bullet took his heart. He had a few moments left and would have tried to jump me if he'd known which way to go. As it was, he stood still and a roar of rage came from his wide open mouth. When the last ounce of air left his lungs he fell and I walked to him.

There were two small calves, mangled bone and flesh. I went back to the mother. She hadn't moved. I felt awfully sorry for her and I told her I was sorry and I shot her. I'd always managed to get a moose for winter meat with no trouble and this should have been wonderful moose country. There was plenty of feed and lots of heavy timber for winter shelter, but there were just too many grizzlies. I believe they killed a good seventy percent of moose calves.

❄ ❄ ❄

The hill by the lake was our observation point. Ann and I were sitting there one day. We could see big lakes in the distance, a high mountain range many miles to the west. An endless stretch of timber lay to the south and to the north was the vast stretch of tundra. I had sat on top of that hill many times, enjoying the peace of everything I saw, and I think that is why I liked that country so much. I was glad

Ann felt the same. On a clear day we could see forever, and sometimes it seemed we weren't more than a step from heaven.

If you live in the wilderness long enough, you develop a sense of awareness that you don't otherwise have. I felt that now. Something was wrong. I had my packboard on my back and my rifle was slung on it. I looked behind me and a wolverine was crouched, not more than twenty feet away from us, crouched low and moving slowly forward. I leaped to my feet and tripped over the stock of my rifle. By the time I got organized, the wolverine was far down the slope. I'll never know what he had in mind. He had crept up on us for a long way, up a flat, open slope. Maybe the breeze was such that he couldn't smell us or maybe he was the rare wolverine that wanted to try. There are always exceptions to rules, and I think this was one of them.

Another exception to the rules occurred later that fall. Wolverine and grizzly simply don't bother one another. They are both ugly, mean and vicious. They both love to kill and they both apparently have the greatest respect for each other.

In this country the grizzly was king. Not a benevolent king but a wayward cruel animal and one of the most powerful on earth. The male will mate and that is the end of his responsibility. I have watched a male grizzly kill and partially eat a small cub, his own. Just something he could kill. Grizzlies love to kill. Not just for food but for pleasure. I have read that there are three basic rules to observe in bear country. Don't disturb a bear while it is feeding. Don't surprise a bear. Don't get between a female and her young. I think there should be four rules. Number one and the most important never to forget is this: Always expect a grizzly to attack. They need absolutely no provocation. It simply depends on how they feel at the time.

All the years I lived in that country I knew where I could go, and where I couldn't. I didn't make a practice of traveling the brush country along the rivers until late fall; by that time, the salmon run is over and the bears are up in open country, feeding on berries. In open country I had the advantage. I had a rifle and knew how to use it. In the open, nearly every grizzly I have had to kill rose to its hind legs when it got close. When they stand up and roar and bellow and click their teeth, they're ready to come in. Then they will be close enough for you to put your shot exactly where you want it.

Just shooting, just hitting a grizzly, won't help you. I have read of an experienced hunter and guide who shot a grizzly sixteen times. A shot through the stomach or the hind quarters would be mortal, eventually. It's just that in the meantime, he will kill you.

A grizzly has only two vital areas that will put it down: the heart and lung area, and the spine. The spine is a difficult shot but a shot there will put a raging grizzly right in your lap. In the brush, on the two occasions when I was attacked, it was an unexpected encounter, head-on and fast. Even so, a chest shot dead center and a couple of inches above the breastbone will slow a bear down. If you need another shot you'll still have time. Put it in the same place, right in the heart, lungs and diaphragm. A bear can't stand up under that kind of punishment.

In the brush, you will have no advantage over a bear. You must use every bit of common sense you have. If you allow yourself to be jumped from the side, your chance of survival isn't good. Check the trail ahead of you. Check every shadow, then check it again. That time I'd gone down the Nuyakuk River looking for old Jake Savolly and was on my way back upriver, I didn't check anything. My mind was on Klutuk when it should have been on the grizzlies, feeding on salmon in the river. The bear that jumped me from the river bank was no more than two feet from the end of my rifle barrel. An article I read later told much the same story: "The grizzly came with unbelievable speed. I didn't even have time to look through the scope. I fired and the heavy slug struck the top of his head. The bear was found the next day, by plane, thirty miles away. It had died from massive brain damage."

Using a rifle scope in the brush is suicide, in my view. Even if you have time to look through a scope in the brush, all you will see is brush. Possibly a large patch of brown fur, but where do you point your rifle? An open sight is the only thing to use on grizzlies. If they are too far away for that, forget about your bear. You'll be much better off.

❄ ❄ ❄

Later in the fall, when the salmon were gone from the river and streams, it was time to start a trapline for mink.

Ann had never seen the river country and she wanted to go with me. I loaded my pack with traps and we set out. Wherever I wanted a mink set I wired a trap to an alder or a willow, anything that was secure, and only laid as many on a line as I could set in one day. We traveled down the river perhaps eight miles, and that was enough. On our way home we followed an old dry wash, a place where the river had run a long time ago. At the end of an open space, not more than thirty feet away, a black fox was standing. I had trapped several cross-foxes but I had never seen a black one. My rifle was slung across the back of my packboard. I didn't want to move too much and Ann was just behind me.

"Ann," I whispered, "hand me the rifle."

"I'll not do it." She didn't whisper, she said it loud and clear.

The fox made a swift move and was gone in the brush.

I turned to her.

"Ann, do you know a hundred and fifty dollars just jumped into that brush?"

"I don't care. I won't let you kill a beautiful thing like that."

She wasn't hardened to the fact that if I wanted a beautiful pelt I had to take the life of the animal that was wearing it. She never would be. Her face was earnest and intense. She had a wonderful soft heart and I had to smile a little.

❊ ❊ ❊

Sometimes an animal will do a thing so strange it's beyond all understanding.

I was in shallow water on the river, not seven feet from the shore, busy making an otter set. I heard a small sound on the bank and looked up. A fox was sitting by my packboard. He was staring at me, his eyes squinting in the bright sun. I asked him what he was doing there and he cocked his head. I finished my set, walked to the bank and sat down by my packboard. We weren't more than three feet from each other. He stared at me with yellow, lambent eyes as though he was telling me something.

"How would you like to come home with me?"

I got to my feet and put the packboard on my shoulders.

"You can come if you want to." I picked up my rifle and walked away. I turned and looked and he was still sitting there, watching me. I went on and I don't know whether it was him I saw again or whether it was the fox on the hill. Once in a while I would get a glimpse of a fox as it disappeared in the brush. One of them may have been him.

❊ ❊ ❊

In the middle of November Ann and I walked up the Tikchik canyon to a place where I knew the cranberries were plentiful. Ann pointed to the ridge above us.

"Fred, what's that black thing up there?"

"Either a burned black stump or a wolverine, and there are no stumps up there."

I sat down and held the sights on the black spot. It was a wolverine's head; the rest of the body was hidden by the deep moss. When I fired, the black shape settled just a bit. I had forgotten to hold low to compensate for the steep uphill slope. I held six inches low on the second shot and the wolverine came tumbling and screaming down the slope and lodged in the brush. We went round him on our way to the top of the canyon and saw him thirty feet below us and not moving. I worked my way down and rolled him over. My bullet had broken his neck but then I saw a place between his shoulders where the hide, flesh, muscles and the tips of his shoulder blades had been scooped out. He had been badly injured and must have crawled to the place where we had first seen him.

Only one thing could have done that much damage to a wolverine—a grizzly bear. Most wolverines I have seen weighed from twenty-five to thirty-five pounds and I've seen one or two that weighed forty. This one, I reckoned, weighed a full sixty pounds. I knew the grizzly he had tangled with hadn't got off without damage. I went back to the top of the ridge and on to the top of a small rise. What I saw didn't surprise me.

A grizzly was standing there, not more than a hundred yards away. He held his head low and was slowly moving it from side to side. I put the binoculars on him and he looked close enough to touch. What I saw was hard to believe. His face was in shreds. His eyes were bloody pulp. His nose was slashed to ribbons. He couldn't see and he couldn't smell. He was helpless and I don't think he had moved ten feet from where the battle had taken place. I moved close and shot him from the side. He went down at once and I think he must have been glad to die. I could never be sure which of them had made the first move but one thing I was sure of: the wolverine had done his work first. At close quarters he'd be much quicker than a grizzly. He would be in and out before the bear could swing on him, his claws slashing like spring-loaded razor blades. The grizzly had made his one lucky grab after he was disabled.

A grizzly and a wolverine are both vicious and cruel but I suppose they are meant to be that way. For the first and only time in my life, I felt a small touch of compassion for them.

❄ ❄ ❄

Snow finally came and winter was with us. I put out my traplines for marten. There was a good marten crossing at the far end of the small lake that joined ours, and I had a set there. I used a few spruce limbs to protect the trap from snow. It looked like a little cubby hole. A few grouse feathers, thrown in the back of the trap, were all that was needed.

I went down that way one morning and saw something I didn't like too well. A small she-wolf was in the trap. She didn't weigh over thirty pounds and she was a beautiful young animal. She wouldn't look at me. She stared off into the timber. I had a .22 rifle in my pack and reached for it. I held it in my hands and I couldn't do it, I couldn't shoot her. I'd told Ann I had too much respect for wolves to trap them and now this had happened in our first winter.

A wolf has a very keen intelligence. This one, by the way she stood and her refusal to look at me, told me that she knew I meant her death, and yet she wouldn't show fear.

I put the rifle back in my pack, turned and headed for the cabin. I kicked my snowshoes off and went inside.

"Ann, fix a cup of coffee for me and put your warm clothes on."

"You haven't been gone long, Fred, what's wrong?"

"About a mile from here there's a young she-wolf in one of my traps. I'm going to turn her loose, and I need your help."

I went out to the windbreak and brought in a coil of narrow rope.

"I'm going to loop this round her neck. There will be no turn in it. I'll just lay it across one side of her neck and you can hold the two ends in your hands. Hold the rope fast and snug. That way she won't be able to turn her head to me.

After I take her foot from the trap, let go one end of the rope. She'll do the rest."

"You're going to get torn to pieces."

"No, I'm not."

Ann got ready and we left the cabin. When we reached the wolf I could see she hadn't moved a muscle. She was standing there, proud and beautiful. I had Ann place herself twenty feet back, took the rope and walked close to the wolf. When I tossed the loop over her neck I don't believe she so much as quivered. I went to Ann and gave her the two ends to hold.

I walked round to the other side of the wolf and took off my snowshoes. I went within two feet of her and turned my back, moving backward till I could feel her shoulder against my legs. I had plenty of thick, heavy clothing on and I knew she couldn't do much damage. I put one of my feet on the chain, close to the trap, I bent down, took the trap and depressed the spring, prying the jaws apart. I took her paw in my hand and pulled it free. Still she didn't move a muscle and I walked away from her.

"Ann, let one end of your rope loose."

Then the wolf moved away and the rope slid from her neck and she was free. She trotted perhaps fifty feet, and stopped. She turned her head and looked at us and I wished I'd tied the rope fast. I believe she would have come home with us. She turned away and I saw the last glimpse of her as she disappeared in the timber.

She was a wolf that had been left behind when all the rest of them had moved out in late fall, and she would have a hard winter.

It was almost Christmas time, and we wanted a tree to brighten our home. We cut down a small spruce about two feet high and trimmed it with the narrow metal strips that come from the tops of coffee cans, the kind you wind off with a key; we stretched them out until they looked like shining cones. We strung some popcorn on a thread and draped that round the tree as well, and it looked fine.

On Christmas Eve we listened to our radio. "Silent Night, Holy Night," all the Christmas carols, came over the air.

Every evening we could pick up personal radio messages from everywhere on the Yukon and Kuskokwim rivers. Someone was injured, or perhaps they were sick, and a radio transmitter was sending an appeal for help. Someone, somewhere, always heard. It might be a doctor in Bethel, or Nome, perhaps Holy Cross. Sometimes a nurse stationed somewhere by the Public Health Service would hear the call and respond. The injury would be described or the symptoms of sickness were discussed, and the treatment for any of these things was given in detail. We learned a lot that way, and also that a call for help was always answered.

❄ ❄ ❄

In the southern states they have a small rabbit. The western states have their jackrabbit. In the northern states, and Alaska, there is the snowshoe hare. In Alaska we also have the almost legendary arctic hare. It will weigh from twenty-five to thirty pounds and, sitting up, it is as high as a medium-sized dog. In the winter time they are pure white with black-tipped ears. They travel the open tundra in large groups and they follow the willow ravines, for willow is their food.

One day in January Ann was outside the cabin, and when she came in her eyes were wide with disbelief.

"Fred, come out here and look!"

I went with her and she pointed toward the trees. He was sitting there and he was a big one. I looked back through the timber and there were two or three more of them.

"Those are arctic hares. Take a good look. They don't come this far south very often. Most people have never seen them."

By the middle of April, when Matt came to pick us up, Ann had experienced many new things, and having her with me to share my life had been wonderful for me. With her there, I looked with new eyes at my world and saw a future where before there had been only a life.

✳ ✳ ✳

Most of the news in Dillingham was news of war. Fighting was raging all over Europe.

I remembered the end of the First World War, when I was a kid. That was the war that would end all wars, and thousands of men gave their lives to bring peace to this earth. Somewhere, the silent voices of the dead must have been crying out in protest.

The United States was shipping war materiel to Great Britain. Food always plays a great part in the ammunition for war, and that summer we fished for salmon twenty-four hours a day, seven days a week. There were no closed periods and no closed areas. We drifted for salmon until the run of fish was over.

Ann and I were late that year getting ready to leave. It was the middle of August before we had everything together.

"Fred, there's something I should tell you. We're going to have a baby."

I put my arms around her and hugged her. "We'll stay in town this winter."

She pushed away from me. "No, Fred, we won't. The baby isn't due till the last week in March. We can have Matt pick us up the last week in February. It will give us plenty of time. I don't want to stay out here this winter."

I didn't try very hard to make her change her mind. Instead I began to make plans for a new cabin. It would be bigger and I would hew out a floor. I'd need an adz for that. Someone in town would have one. Heine Hildebrandt used to do a lot of work on cabins. He ran a small restaurant now and I went to see him. He told me he had what I needed, and he'd bring it with him the next morning. As I was getting up to leave I saw a man back in the kitchen.

"Isn't that John Shipton?"

Heine nodded. "Yes, that's John."

I called to him, "John?" and he looked up and came to the counter.

"Yes?"

"John, did you ever think of going back to the Tikchiks? We used to be partners."

There was a distressed look in his eyes.

"No, Mr. Hatfield, that must have been someone else. I've always lived here."

"Oh. Yes, of course."

I motioned for Heine to come with me and I stepped outside.

"What's happened to him?"

"They did a frontal lobectomy on his brain at the institution. They took away his memory. He doesn't remember now that he used to be afraid."

"But he remembered the way I looked. He remembered my name."

"Well, you played quite a part in his life, Fred. You found him up in that country and you brought him down the rivers. You and he were together a long time. You're in a place in his mind somewhere."

"They shouldn't have done that to him. I still think if they had given it longer, maybe things would have worked out."

I went back for the adz the next morning and we left town about ten o'clock on a beautiful clear day. Two miles from Spruce Lake I happened to look in the sky above the plane. There was a mountain range there, standing out so clearly I could see the timber on it. I tapped Matt on the shoulder and pointed up.

He nodded. "I've seen that several times, always close to this area."

Ann looked at me, her face filled with wonder. I thought of old Peetla and I thought of Frank Waskey and his theory of refracted images, of a focal point.

There was no grizzly reaching up for the plane this time. Matt made his approach and landed. He pulled the plane to the shore and we all got out and walked to the cabin. It was standing strong and firm. There was just one thing wrong. A big corner of the roof had been demolished, the same place as the year before.

"Fred, the same grizzly does that every year."

"I know. I'm building a new cabin this fall. It'll be farther down the lake and maybe he'll leave it alone. If you've ever noticed, there's a bear trail right across the front of us. Perhaps that's what the trouble is."

Matt left us and went off for the second load, saying he'd make it back as soon as he could. We'd finished carrying our things to the cabin and were cutting hay for the bed when we heard his plane coming in.

Everything unloaded, Matt announced: "I've got plenty of time. I'm going to help you and Ann get things in shape before I leave."

Matt never failed to have plenty of time and we were glad to have his help. He knew Ann was pregnant and we told him again to be sure and pick us up in the latter part of February.

✣ ✣ ✣

I had promised Ann a new cabin and I picked a spot halfway down the lake where the timber was straight and the trees were the right size.

Building a cabin isn't too difficult if you fell your trees the right way. I dropped mine in a straight line and limbed them, then moved over ten feet and dropped another line the same way. Starting at the far end I used the two lines of logs as a rollway to the cabin site. In another stand of good trees I did the same thing, laying down one round of logs, and then I went to work on the cabin floor, hewing the logs flat on all four sides and notching them to fit the crosspieces I had laid. Our new cabin was fourteen by eighteen feet, so the floor was a real undertaking. After I had all the logs hewn and laid in place, I took the adz and made them smooth. That floor took me two weeks to finish, but when I was done we had a floor we could sweep and keep clean. By the middle of October, everything was done. I had put up a new cache, too, and all our winter supplies were moved from the old location.

The weather turned chilly and it was time to get our winter's meat. I left one morning and followed the timberline toward the canyon, the same old game trail. I got to the edge of the canyon and below the slope I saw a nice-sized bull moose. His head was low and he was walking real slow. I shot him through the neck. Most moose shot that way will walk a few steps or perhaps make a half turn before they fall. This one went down at once.

I walked down to him and once I had him skinned I understood why he'd looked so tired. His chest was a solid bruise and one side of his rib cage had been punctured by the tine of an antler of another moose. He'd been in a battle with another bull, and lost. He'd been drawing air through the hole in his ribs and I don't believe he would have been able to go much further. I cut the meat into pieces I could handle and hung them from a tree. Carrying what I could on my pack-board, I went home.

We listened to our radio that evening and it wasn't the cheerful thing it used to be. The war was spreading and more nations were involved; it was as though the world was ruled by a handful of men who were insane.

Ann insisted on going with me the next day to help me pack our meat home. We left early and were at the canyon edge just as the sun was breaking over the horizon. I looked up the canyon and four hundred yards away a moose was standing. He was between two trees and his antlers reached from tree to tree, the sun causing them to shine like gold above a coat as black as night. He was a magnificent monster. I pointed him out to Ann. "That's worth getting up early in the morning to see, isn't it?"

The words were barely out of my mouth when he came. He came like a racehorse and his pounding hoofs striking the frozen earth sounded like the beat of a hundred drums. I reached for my rifle and my heart dropped like a stone as I realized I hadn't brought it with me. I'd thought it would just be in my way—the grizzlies were up in the hills and I'd have no need for it. It was a bad mistake but I'd made it.

There were a few small tundra spruce behind us. It would have been easy to place your hand round one of them and snap a squirrel out of the top, they were that small, but they had to do.

We hustled to them and threw our packboards off. I boosted Ann up into one of them and I climbed another five feet away and we didn't have long to wait. Never before and never since that time have I seen a moose that approached him in size. He came to the base of Ann's tree and pawed the ground. Ann had a red jacket tucked under the tie rope of her packboard. He saw that and hooked it with his antlers and tossed it twenty feet away with an impatient shake of his head. He turned, then, and went down the slope.

Ann looked over to me and I shook my head. Soon we heard him coming up the slope again for one last look. A moose doesn't have good eyesight and he'd thought we were just one more moose. A bull or cow, it didn't matter. He was ready to fight or mate, whichever came first. This was the bull that had given the one I had shot such a terrific beating.

He turned again and went down the slope. We stayed where we were for a little while, then I climbed down from my haven of safety and walked carefully to the edge of the canyon. Nothing was in sight and I couldn't hear a sound. He was gone.

I went to Ann and helped her down from her tree. We went back to the edge of the canyon and watched for a while longer and listened. I went down to where our meat was hanging and tied a load on my packboard. We went home, then, and Ann decided she'd had enough for that day. I made several trips and finally got our meat home. My rifle went with me, as it did in all the years after that, whenever I left the cabin.

8 / *War in the Wilderness*

It was December now. As the seasons changed, so did our activities. Mink trapping was over and I was ready for the marten lines. One morning Ann and I were sitting at the table. The radio was turned on and we were listening to the weather and the local news, out of Anchorage. The announcer broke off his talk with these words: "This is a special broadcast. The Japanese have bombed Pearl Harbor."

I'm not sure what we said. Probably nothing for a time. I think that when you hear words that are unbelievable, words that shock your mind, it takes a while to realize that what you've heard is the truth.

It was still early at Pearl Harbor. Almost everyone was sleeping, for it was Sunday. The Japanese bombers came in low. They came in at dawn. When they were finished, our Pacific fleet was badly crippled and more than two thousand men were dead. The following day Germany and Italy declared war on the United States.

Ann and I were isolated from the rest of the world but even so all of this had an effect on us. Our thoughts and our talk to one another were dictated day after day by the continuing news of war. Suddenly trapping seemed a futile and useless thing. We stayed close by our radio. Russia, across the water, was at war with Germany and so far Japan had made no hostile move northward against its erstwhile adversary, or against Alaskan territory.

We had a warm January thaw and the surface of the snow turned soft. Then the weather became cold again; at night it might be forty below. The snow had a hard solid crust now and we could walk on it without snowshoes.

It was January 19. Ann and I were walking around through the trees. It was good to be out like this, relaxed in fresh, crisp air. Suddenly Ann broke through the crust with one leg and called to me for help. I went over and saw her face was pale and drawn. She was hurt. I knew I'd have to carry her and her weight and mine combined would cause me to go through the snow's surface too.

"I'll have to go back for my snowshoes."

I couldn't seem to move fast enough, fumbling and hurrying, a cold sort of fear beginning to grow inside me. I picked her up in my arms and carried her back. I laid her on the bed and removed her clothes and then I saw why she was helpless and in pain: the water sack surrounding her baby had ruptured. The baby wasn't due to be born for more than two months and my feeling of dread and helplessness took hold.

"Fred, what are we going to do?" Her words forced me to think. She was waiting for me to come up with an answer.

"Listen to me. There are people living all through the Wood River lakes. I can be there in two days. Someone will have a dog team, we can get into Dillingham and I'll have a plane back here within three days."

"No, Fred, please don't leave me."

We talked it over. We weren't sure what might happen while I was gone. I stayed.

Ann was in constant pain. The next day she was tired and worried.

"Fred, this will be a dry birth. Our baby will be born in a very few days or it won't be born."

"Don't worry, I'll do something."

I was helpless and all I could do was be there with her. The second and third day passed and then the fourth. By the fifth day Ann was semiconscious. I made a crib out of an empty evaporated milk carton. I took an eye-dropper and boiled its rubber bulb so that it would stretch over the open end of a small vanilla extract bottle. I cut two pieces of string to use on the umbilical cord.

The next few days were days of despair. Ann was comatose and didn't know me. For the first time in my life, I knew real fear.

The tenth night was cold; it may have been fifty below. I kept the cabin warm for Ann and stepped outside for a breath of air. It was just after midnight. The stars were brilliant and seemed so close I felt I might almost touch them.

I looked beyond the stars into the far-off heavens.

"Lord, I've never asked you for much. I do now. Will you help us?"

The answer came so surely it was as though He'd been waiting, patiently waiting, just for me to ask.

I heard a baby cry.

I ran to the cabin and hurried to Ann. The baby's head was out of its mother. I felt inside and I could feel the tiny shoulders. I helped the baby out and it was born. It was in this big world now. It was still crying and I knew it was all right. I looked at Ann and her eyes were open.

"Fred, do we have our baby?"

"Yes, honey, a beautiful baby."

I wasn't sure who to help first. I tied the umbilical cord in two places and cut between the pieces of string. I had hot water on the stove and I cooled some of it and washed the baby. I filled the vanilla bottle, half evaporated milk and half water, and added a little corn syrup. The baby was a little girl and she went to work on the nipple I had made. She seemed just fine. Patricia Ann, born January 30 at 12:30 A.M. Place of birth, Spruce Lake, in the Tikchik country.

I knew there was an afterbirth. Ann couldn't help me so I wrapped the cord round my hand and gently pulled. It resisted at first and then I could feel it begin to give. I pulled steadily and it came easily enough, a round hard ball that had served its purpose, and I carried it outside. The long days of hopeless despair were over.

I took care of Ann. I washed her and put some pillows behind her shoulders. After ten long days in bed she was glad to sit up. I brought her baby to her and all the love in the world was in her eyes. After three more days Ann was on her feet and the baby was in her care. It didn't seem possible that she was so well now, after the hard days she had survived.

In the middle of February we heard the sound of a plane in the distance and a short time later Matt had landed. He had a passenger with him, a man dressed in uniform. I don't remember his name, but he was a major in the United States Air Force.

Matt was surprised to see Ann with her baby and we told him what had happened.

"I don't know where you're going from here, Matt, but as soon as you can, come back and pick us up. Both Ann and the baby need things we don't have."

"Sure, sure. Listen, Fred, the major seems to think you have company in here."

It was a strange statement and I waited for the major to explain.

"Matt tells me you cover this country pretty well?"

"I did until December 7 and Pearl Harbor. Since then we've stayed here, listening to war news."

"Did you see any snowshoe trails or hear any planes land?"

"No, there's been nothing. There is no one in here except us."

"Well, we've pinpointed this area as the source of a daily weather report sent out to Japanese ships. Someone in here has a very efficient transmitter. Do you mind if I take a look at your radio? It's part of my job."

I shook my head. "Help yourself."

He took our radio off the shelf and looked it over, and went outside and looked at our antenna.

When he came back in our cabin, I had a question.

"Major, just how did you pick this area? There's a lot of country north of here."

"We used triangulation. When it comes to distance and location, it's precise and exact. Don't be surprised if you see a flight of planes covering this area."

I wanted so much to tell him that this was a strange valley, that objects were seen and sounds heard that didn't really happen, though they seemed to. I knew he would simply think it a far-out, impossible story. I turned instead to Matt.

"There are quite a few people living on the Kuskokwim, around Aniak. There's no one closer than that."

Five days later Matt was back to pick us up and he told us the major had found his man not far from Aniak. He was a Japanese American and, as the major had said, he was equipped with a very efficient radio transmitter. What did surprise the major, with his triangulation know-how, was that he was a hundred miles north of us.

❈ ❈ ❈

Dillingham had changed. All the single men who were young enough had been drafted or had enlisted. Most of them were formed into a body of men named the "Alaska Scouts" and played an important role in that part of the war that was close to Alaska.

From past neglect, Alaska had no defense of any kind against invasion by Japan, but the attack on Pearl Harbor caused the United States to realize that Alaska was an open corridor for the invasion of Canada and the United States.

To facilitate troop movements in March 1942 construction of a highway began, linking Canada and Alaska. Work started simultaneously in three separate places and that summer it was finished, over fifteen hundred miles of graveled highway through unbroken wilderness. Sixty miles from Dillingham, at King Salmon, construction of a runway for United States Air Force fighters and bombers was begun and finished that summer too.

In early June 1942 the Japanese bombed Unalaska and Dutch Harbor, less than five hundred miles from Dillingham. On June 12, 1942, the Japanese took Alaska's Aleutian islands of Kiska and Attu. The war had moved much closer to us. Fishing for salmon was wide open again that summer. We fished around the clock, seven days a week, till the run ended.

The previous winter had been rough on Ann and I didn't really expect her to have any enthusiasm for the Tikchiks. If she wanted to, I was ready to winter in Dillingham, but the big lake country had worked its spell. She wanted to go back.

When Matt landed with the first load and we walked to our new cabin, we had a pleasant surprise. The roof hadn't been touched, so the roll of canvas I'd brought with me wasn't needed. Matt brought in our second load of supplies and before he left he had a good suggestion.

"Meat's hard to come by in Dillingham now. You and Ann are each entitled to a moose. Why don't you get two this fall and bring one out with you in the spring? What you don't need, plenty of other people will."

"Okay, we'll do it. I'll wait till freeze-up and have the meat ready to take out with us."

Matt left us and we got busy. We had brought a collapsible crib for the baby and getting the cabin set up was our first priority. Ann was a mother now and there would be no more setting traplines for her.

The second day of December was rainy. It had been a late fall and I was still waiting for the weather to get cold before I went hunting for moose. There was a pool on the Tikchik that held lake trout, rainbows, grayling and Dolly Varden, so we wouldn't go hungry. I put on my rain gear, took my rifle and fishing rod and headed for the river. Six inches of snow on the ground made sloppy walking. I came out on the edge of a large open place in the timber. On the far side stood a female grizzly and her two two-year-olds.

Rain was pouring down. I had a hard rain hat on and it sounded as though I was standing under a tin roof. I stood still. The old sow let out a loud grunt when she saw me and all three bears moved toward me. I sat on a hummock and waited. She should have driven the two-year-olds off in the fall but she hadn't. I was sure she would leave after she looked me over but she didn't.

Being challenged by a grizzly never becomes a routine. Every encounter is like the first time, for they are awesome antagonists. She came closer and stood up. A few loud roars and she dropped down again and moved closer. The two-year-olds nipped at her heels and she swiped at them. They seemed to be telling her, "Go get him." She was telling them that this was her job and she'd do it her way.

I still hoped she might leave me alone but when she was about seventy yards away she stood up again, dropped down again and moved closer. She was making a steady roaring and bellowing noise and I knew she was serious. I was ready for her and when she stood up again thirty yards away I knew it was time and I fired.

She went over backward and was hidden from sight behind a high knoll. The two-year-olds made for the timber to my left: I could hear branches being ripped down and a steady roaring from the bears. I wasn't sure that the female hadn't got up and gone into the brush with the others. I was in the best spot I could be so I sat right where I was.

After about twenty minutes I walked carefully to where the female had gone down. She was lying on her back, all four feet in the air, and she was very dead. At that moment the two-year-olds broke out of the brush and headed across the opening in a wild rush. I fired a shot over their backs to hurry them along, then I opened up the sow to see what my bullet had done. I carried a .30–06 rifle and had used a 220-grain bullet. The heavy slug had taken her through the heart, lungs and diaphragm.

I sat down for a time. This confrontation had got me a little wound up and I needed to pull myself together. After a while I continued on to the river, caught some rainbow trout and took them home. Everything was late that fall. The river was still open and bears were still roaming around.

❄ ❄ ❄

The weather finally turned cold and when I'd provided for us I looked for a moose to take out in the spring. I wanted a big one and I found him. I believe he weighed over twelve hundred pounds and I know he provided at least six hundred pounds of good meat. It was going to be a welcome change of diet for the families who had wintered in Dillingham. I trapped that winter in a halfhearted way. War news took precedence over everything else and when Matt came in the middle of March to pick us up, we were ready to leave.

When we landed at Dillingham, we loaded everything in Matt's pickup, only stopping long enough at our cabin to get the oil stove going and to leave our personal things. Ann and our baby came to the trading store with us, for it would take a while for the cabin to warm up. Matt and I took the moose meat and hung it in Tubby's big freezer.

The next day Ann and I were still getting our cabin in shape. We had bought a stock of groceries and it was taking a little time to get settled down. There was a knock on the door and I went to it. It was Larson, the game warden, and I asked him to come in.

"No, Fred, this is official business. I understand you brought a moose out with you. Do you mind if I have a look at it?"

Larson had me puzzled, but I told him to wait while I got my coat on.

We walked to the trading store and I took him to the freezer. He looked the meat over and turned to me.

"You know, Fred, the law states that moose meat must retain evidence of sex until it has reached a place of consumption. There's nothing on this meat that tells me whether it's a cow or a bull and I'm afraid that doesn't satisfy the law."

He walked out and I went home. I knew he wasn't through with me. Two days later he came to our cabin again.

"Fred, I have authority from the game department in Juneau to seize that meat."

I made a mistake then. I should have realized that any authority he had from Juneau would have been a radio message and I could have demanded to see it. I didn't. I took him to the meat locker and he carried out my meat and loaded it on the back of a truck. There were eleven pieces. I counted each one.

The next day I was in the trading store and John Bradshaw walked in. He had been the U.S. Marshal for a year and he was a good one.

"Fred, I'm sorry but I've got a warrant from the commissioner for your arrest."

I wasn't entirely unprepared for what was taking place. The appointment of U.S. commissioners had done very little to ensure legal justice for Alaska's people, especially in remote areas. I didn't know where the present one came from but I did know he was Larson's cousin. In Dillingham the commissioner was the law, judge and jury, but none of them had any legal training. The equipment allowing them to dispense justice was simply a book listing the various offenses and affixing various penalties. The penalty for each offense had a wide range of severity, from lenient to rather harsh. In my case I knew it meant one or two months in jail and a stiff fine.

"John, I need about three hours. Could you hold off until two o'clock?"

"I can do that, Fred. I'll see you at the commissioner's court at two."

The army now had a signal corps close to the hospital, consisting of Sergeant Bill Withrow, his wife and their two children. I knew Withrow well enough: I'd helped him erect a high antenna tower for his radio transmitter. Now he could send a message anywhere in Alaska. I drove over there in Tubby's pickup and told him about my problem.

Judge Tony Diamond held court in Anchorage. He was a firm man, an eminent jurist, and he was honest. Diamond High School and Diamond Boulevard were named after him.

I wrote out a message and handed it to Bill.

Judge Tony Diamond
Anchorage, Alaska

I had moose meat in a private cold storage locker. It was seized by the area game warden, Carlos Larson, for not having evidence of sex. I am to appear in commissioner's court at two o'clock this afternoon for trial. I need your help.

Sincerely,
Fred Hatfield
Dillingham, Alaska

"Bill, I think you'll get a reply to this. When you do, could you bring it into town? You'll probably find me in the commissioner's court."

I went back to town then and at two o'clock I was in court. Larson was the prosecutor.

"Your honor, I charge this man with being in possession of moose meat not having evidence of sex."

"Larson, I took that moose after freeze-up last winter. That's been a long time."

"That's contempt of court, your honor."

The commissioner's gavel came down with a thump.

"That's contempt. Proceed, Mr. Larson."

"Your honor, according to the game regulations, a moose must retain evidence of sex until it has reached a place of consumption. This was not done."

"Larson, you could twist that around so that it would mean my own dinner table."

"Contempt of court, your honor."

"That's contempt." Down with the gavel.

I heard the door open and close and I turned. Bill Withrow was walking toward us with papers in his hand. He gave one to me, handed one to the commissioner and one to Larson. I read mine.

Fred Hatfield
Dillingham, Alaska

Moose meat that has been placed in storage need contain no evidence of sex. Your meat was seized illegally and will be returned to you within three hours. I have sent a message to the commissioner and one to the game warden, Carlos Larson. I will write a letter to the Dept. of Game at Juneau.

Judge Tony Diamond
Anchorage, Alaska

The faces of the commissioner and the game warden were classic studies of dismay. It was as though Judge Diamond was there in the court room, pointing an accusing finger at them. When the commissioner was able to speak, his voice was a bare whisper: "This case is dismissed."

Larson brought my meat back that afternoon and hung it from where he had taken it.

After a week, the commissioner was replaced and in less than a month Larson was transferred to Seward. The families who had wintered in Dillingham had their moose meat.

At that time, it's quite true, the regulation regarding the taking of a moose read: "Moose meat must retain evidence of sex until it has reached a place of consumption." The taking of a cow moose was illegal and this ruling meant that the testicles of a bull had to be left attached to one of the hindquarters, even on a meat rack in the Tikchiks. But I had the meat in storage and Larson had chosen to interpret that regulation to suit his purpose. The following year the regulation was changed to read: "Moose meat shall retain evidence of sex until it has reached a place of storage." It was Judge Tony Diamond's ruling almost to the letter.

❊　❊　❊

That spring American and Canadian forces recaptured the Aleutian island of Attu and in August the Japanese evacuated the island of Kiska. It was 1943 and the tides of war were slowly turning in favor of the Allies.

For Ann and Patricia and me, August was time to leave town, time for us to go home. When I recall it now, it seems almost impossible that we would think of the big lake country as home, but we did.

Our new cabin was in fine shape. Perhaps the grizzlies had realized that no matter what they did, we would still come back. In all the following years that we lived in the lake country, they never bothered one of our cabins again.

Having a baby with us seemed to make time pass quickly. Our radio still gave us all the war news. Japan, Germany and Italy knew now that they faced a grim, determined world, that slowly but surely they were losing.

When the nights turned cold and frosty I knew the moose would start their mating season. I had learned how to call moose. I had heard a cow talk to a bull so many times I could imitate her well enough to fool a bull. If there was one within a mile of me I knew he'd hear me call, and I knew he'd come.

I didn't go far from our cabin. I walked up through the timber to the game trail that followed the tundra edge and picked a spot that had the right kind of trees for a good cross-pole to hang the meat from. I called three or four times at spaced intervals, and waited.

I saw him coming, saw him stop and reach down with his antlers and hook them into the tundra moss. He brought his head up and shook the moss away. I grunted a short, low sound and he came. When he was not more than thirty yards away, I shot him. He was a good big bull and by the time I had the meat hung, it was time to go home. I took the liver with me and it was almost dark by the time I reached our cabin. Ann had heard the shot and she had the frying pan hot on the stove. Ours was surely a fine way to live.

Next morning we had an early breakfast and I left. Getting the meat home wouldn't be hard but it was going to take a while. I reached the timberline and where my meat had been hanging there was a broken pole, dangling from one of the trees.

I backed carefully away and moved out on to the open tundra for a hundred yards. I knew what was there in the brush. A grizzly had ripped the pole down and my meat had been carried a few yards and covered with leaves and moss. Each piece would be in a different spot and the bear would be in there too, watching me. That was his meat and he meant to keep it. It was a standoff, for I knew that meat was mine and I intended to have it.

A grizzly has a certain amount of patience but it wears thin rather quickly and then he gets very angry. It started, finally, with a low, guttural growl. I heard some brush snap and a roar of rage and fury. I saw the brush go down and that gave me the right direction. He didn't hesitate. He came for me like the thousand pounds of mad grizzly he was. I fired into his chest once and then again. Neither of my shots went quite where I wanted them—the rough tundra made him a difficult target—but they slowed him down. The third shot took him when he was fifty feet from me and he went down and didn't move. I replaced the shells I had fired and sat where I was for a while.

All this took place near enough to the cabin for Ann to hear the shots, and I could hear her when she shouted for me. I hollered as loud as I could and set off for the cabin. I had to let her see that I was all right.

"It's okay, a grizzly stole our meat and got mad because I wouldn't let him have it."

I sat down at the table and she poured some coffee for me.

"Fred, I'm getting now so I worry about you a lot. Sometimes when you're away I can't help imagining things. I'm almost afraid that someday you won't be coming home."

Ann was pregnant again but this time the baby wasn't due until June.

"You know better than that. You worry too much and you don't have to."

As I held her in my arms and spoke the words, the same thoughts she had spoken were in my mind. I'd known a few good men who hadn't come home. What if some day I didn't come home? Ann would have a difficult time. One of these years I'd have to find something else to do. I'd have to quit this wilderness life. Just the thought of giving up the life we had in this country pushed everything else away.

I went back for our meat. The four quarters and the sides weren't hard to find and other than a huge tooth mark here and there, the bear hadn't damaged it. I finally had all of it packed home.

❊ ❊ ❊

Patty was two years old. She and her mother were alone a lot and for some time she'd been able to talk like a little magpie, so Ann didn't lack for company. All winter our radio had given us the war news. Italy had fallen apart, and the Japanese were being slowly pushed back. When spring arrived and Matt came in to get us, we were glad to see him. The war had made us anxious to get out to the coast where we could talk to people and be closer to things.

Our second baby was born on June 5, 1944. It was a lot easier for Ann this time, in the hospital. We had another girl and we named her Nancy.

Henry Rhoel and I fished together again, and again it was a round-the-clock thing. We fished salmon every day and night till the run was over, till July 25. Two days later American forces recaptured the island of Guam and, almost a year later, in June 1945, the first casualty of the war we had seen came to Dillingham.

Her name was Angela and she was sixteen. After she stepped off the plane at the small airstrip it wasn't more than an hour before everyone in town had heard about her and they moved to help her.

Angela had been born and lived on the tiny island of Attu, taken by the Japanese in 1942.

"They came ashore at daybreak. They came ashore so fast, in small power boats. We could see their ship, anchored out at sea. We could hear explosions and guns firing. None of us knew what was taking place.

"I got separated from my family and was put on a ship. There was still shooting. I could hear it as I was taken away.

After a few days the ship we were on pulled anchor and we traveled for a long time. When we finally dropped anchor again, we were off the island of Guam.

"I was on Guam for two years. The girls who had been with me simply disappeared. Day after day I was treated like an animal and time didn't mean anything, for I knew nothing would change.

"In 1944 it seemed as though the whole world was being blown up, and then the Americans came ashore. The Marines found me and they took me away and I was put on board a hospital ship. We finally came to the United States and they kept me in a hospital for a long while. When it was time for me to leave this spring I told them I wanted to go back to Attu. I wanted to go home. They said there was no one there now. No one except American troops. I guess it was then I knew about the shooting, the morning the Japanese took me away.

"I had left my father and mother and my brother there. All of the people I had ever known lived on Attu. There weren't many of us."

Germany surrendered that spring of 1945, and Japan on September 2. The war had lasted six years and one day.

In the spring of 1946 all the men who had left for the war came home. Most of them had been in the Alaska Scouts and some of them had taken part in the recapture of Attu. I knew Gene Balcom had been there, and he told me what it had been like.

"We moved on the island from opposite sides. It was as though we were two big waves. The Japs were well entrenched and we lost quite a lot of men but when we met in the middle of the island, it was all over. Attu is a barren, windy place and the people lived in sod houses, rounded on top. I went inside three of them. It was the same thing in each one. The people had been lined up around the earth walls. They had been in a sitting position. Some of them had fallen over and some of them were still sitting where they had been shot. They were clothed skeletons. There were mothers who had been holding their children.

"I was one of the lucky ones. I was with the bunch they shipped out. I was glad to leave."

Dr. Salazar was transferred that summer of 1946 and another doctor came to take his place. He was Dr. John Libby and he took charge of the hospital.

Dr. Libby saw Angela in town one day and for both of them it must have caused a surge of memories. He had been a Marine medic when Guam was recaptured. He was the doctor who had treated and cared for Angela.

They had met for the first time thousands of miles away on the island of Guam and their second meeting was in the small village of Dillingham on the Bering Sea coast.

9 / Changes

THE GOVERNOR OF ALASKA was appointed by the President of the United States. He represented the President and the federal interest in the territory, therefore most of the federal agencies came under his hand, including the Department of Fish and Wildlife. Federal authority didn't seem to extend as far west as Bristol Bay, however, and as a consequence conservation of the world's greatest salmon fisheries was ignored.

In order to increase their salmon catch, the canneries had in the past, before my time, completely blocked the rivers with their nets. This stopped almost all spawning, the only source of future salmon runs, and eventually they realized what it meant, and the practice was stopped. The Alaskan salmon industry still controlled Bristol Bay, with little or no interference from the federal government. They controlled the use of sailboats, they controlled the price of fish, they controlled most of the region's economy. Every spring a cannery ship arrived from Seattle and dropped anchor off the mouth of the Nushagak river. It carried supplies for the trading stores and the canneries. Barges would set out for the ship, returning with thousands of cases of empty cans, cans that would be filled with salmon that summer. The ship was eagerly awaited by everyone. It also carried a big supply of

153

fresh fruit and vegetables, the first we had seen since the fall ship nine months before.

The cannery ship never arrived until June, but in 1951 a ship dropped anchor offshore in the middle of May. As we watched, we saw a boat being lowered over the side. In a matter of minutes, it was tied up at the trading store dock. Quite a few of us were on hand as a man climbed the short ladder and stood on the dock. He was Frank Shield, superintendent of Peninsula Packers.

I could see cases of oranges and apples stacked on the deck, and I saw the power roller fastened to the stern. This was a fishing boat but it was a power boat.

"If you men will get those cases of fruit up on the dock I imagine the kids in town will go for it. If you want to take a look at the boat, help yourselves."

It was hard to believe what we found on board. A safety rail was round the deck. There was a place in the stern for salmon and nets. Down below deck there was a small cooking galley, and there were bunks where you could sleep in comfort. There was no sail. It was powered by a Chris Craft motor.

"There are thirty of these boats on the deck of that ship out there. I need sixty men to handle them."

I don't have to say I signed my name. Every man there did the same and in less than an hour I believe every kid in town was trying to peel an orange and chew an apple at the same time.

Peninsula Packers operated a freezer ship: the fresh-caught salmon were cleaned and frozen on board. It was the first of many freezer ships to come into Bristol Bay. For the first time the Alaskan salmon industry had competition. When their ships arrived, the decks were loaded with power boats, too, but for them the Golden Age of Greed was over.

The small cannery cemeteries weren't needed anymore. Grass and weeds grew up around the wooden crosses and after a time it was difficult to find where they had been. In a few short years the big shore canneries of the Alaskan salmon industry weren't operating. They were through and no one mourned their passing.

❄ ❄ ❄

I sat on the lake shore and watched them. They were diving and surfacing and laughing. They were like seals in the water, Ann and her girls. Patty was eleven, Nancy was nine and Sharon was seven. John was sitting on the shore with me. He was a year old.

August had been a warm month, and for Ann and the girls swimming was almost an everyday thing. All the lakes in this country had been gouged out by glaciers a long time ago. There was a small glacial moraine behind me, about eight feet high, extending almost the full length of the lake.

I heard a sound behind me, a short, low grunt, and I knew what it meant. I took my rifle and eased up to the top of the small ridge and looked beyond. A grizzly was there, standing on his hind legs, his head moving from side to side as he tested the air. He was in a bad spot for us, more than fifty yards back but between us and the cabin.

Ann had watched me as I crawled up the small slope and they were quiet in the water. As I crept back to the beach they swam quietly to shore. I took Ann's arm and whispered to her.

"Pick up John, and if you have to, put your hand over his mouth to keep him quiet. You and the girls head down the shore and don't make any noise. Get to the cabin. I'll keep an eye on our visitor."

She didn't waste any time. I eased back up to the top of the ridge, and watched him. Just as Ann and the kids reached the short trail leading to the cabin, he started to move toward the lake shore, and I headed for home. As I reached the cabin trail, he was on the beach and he saw me and started to cover the ground in huge bounds. I ran for the cabin. I wasn't in any danger, for I had a good start on him and I never kill an animal unless I have to. I believe he simply wondered what was going on.

I made it to the cabin just as he reached our trail. He slowed to a walk but he kept coming, moving toward us.

"Ann, get some pans and things and bang them together. Maybe he'll go away."

I think the strange noise and all the new smells from the cabin made up his mind. Huffing and grunting, he turned away from our trail. I stepped away from the cabin a little and watched him as he went over the end of the hill, by the lake.

That evening, after the kids were in bed, Ann and I were sitting outside the cabin, using chairs I had made. It was a habit with us if the weather was fine.

"I was watching you and the girls today, swimming in the lake. Patty's almost as tall as you are. In a few short years our girls will be almost grown up and you know what I'll be, just another old trapper. All our kids know is this lake country. Every summer they have a short time out on the coast, and all they ever see are fishermen and trappers. Most of them are fine men, but our girls need to see other places. All they know is what we've taught them. I've thought about it for quite a while, and it's always been someday. It isn't someday anymore. This is our last year in here."

I looked at Ann and there was a little smile on her face.

"I knew when the time came, when you were ready, you'd tell me. Have you thought about where we'll go, where you'll take us?"

"I've been thinking about the Kenai Peninsula. There are several small towns there and there'll be good schools. It's good moose country, too, and I've heard there are even some farms there. We wouldn't go hungry. I can find something, some kind of work."

When I spoke about finding work, of doing what some other man told me to, there was a sick feeling in me but I put it out of my mind.

Later that fall, the girls were outside. It was just after dusk. They had been told many times to stay close by the cabin and now they came running inside.

"Daddy, the wolves are out there."

"I know, I can hear them."

"Well, Daddy, why are they howling like that?"

"You kids have heard them before and you know they're just talking. They probably wonder what we're doing here. You see, this is their land and they live here most all their lives. You run along and go outside. Stay close and they won't bother you."

I wonder how many girls have had to hurry from the danger of a grizzly, how many have heard the wild song of wolves? Perhaps my girls' younger years in that country weren't wasted after all.

Time went by quickly that winter. I knew I'd never follow another trapline. I knew I'd never travel another trail again, and spring came too soon. When Matt came in to pick us up, all I took with me was my rifle. Ann and the kids took a few things they wanted but everything else was left there. When we flew over the big lakes I wondered if I'd ever see them again. This had been my home for a long time.

I got Ann and the kids settled in town. I didn't intend to fish that summer, for I knew I'd need all the time there was to find a new place for my family, and have the kids ready for school that fall.

I had never really been afraid of anything I could see but when I boarded the small plane that was going to take me to Anchorage I knew a feeling of uncertainty, for I hadn't the slightest idea in this world what I was going to do. I knew I had to find a home for my family, and that somehow I had to make a living for them.

❄ ❄ ❄

"Ann, do you see that flat place over there? The ground slopes away in three places. It has good drainage. We're going to build a full concrete basement there. And on top of the basement, we're going to build a house, a house with a lot of big picture windows."

I looked at Ann, and that little familiar smile was on her face.

When I had left Ann in Dillingham in 1954, I had finally made my way to Homer on the Kenai Peninsula. I had filed on five acres of federal land and it was ours. I had found work with the Homer Electric Company, and after five years now I was crew foreman.

While I talked with Ann about the fine house we were going to have, we were standing in front of our cabin, eight miles out of Homer on the "Old Highway."

Homer was a small, beautiful little town nestled against the shore of Cook Inlet, but the Homer Spit was better—a narrow strip of land, four miles long, extending into the water like a finger, pointing at a high mountain range across Kachemak Bay. We had found a wonderful place to live.

It took us four years to finish our house but it was just the way I'd told Ann it would be. Even her kitchen had two big picture windows. I had lived in a log cabin, one place or another, for thirty years and Ann had lived in one with me for twenty-five.

When we moved into our new home, everyone had their own room. It was like living in a mansion.

❄ ❄ ❄

By 1963, our three older girls were gone. They had finished high school in Homer, they were married and living outside, in the States. John was eleven years old. Frank was nine—he had been born in August, the year we came to Homer—and

Cathy had been born in 1962 soon after we moved into our house.

Ann took a great interest in the Alaskan Crippled Children's Association. She attended all the local meetings and went to every one of the state conventions. Eventually, she was elected vice president of the association. Life was full and satisfying for all of us.

It was the latter part of June, late at night and the three kids were in bed. Ann and I were sitting in the living room. The moon was bright that night and we had the lights turned low. From where we were sitting, we could look out of the big windows that faced the road and see the Caribou Hills.

We saw the red glow against the sky. Streamers of flame shot into the air as trees were ignited. There was a fire on West Hill.

We got into our car and drove toward town. Two miles took us to the West Hill road and we turned up there. A short drive further and we stopped at the top to look. We could see the fire below us: a long stretch of timber was burning and the fire was crawling up the slope, toward the road, burning the dry grass.

As we watched, they came out of the smoky haze, two moose calves in front of their mother, trying to keep moving up the hill, away from the fire. She stayed behind them, urging them on, making sure one of them didn't lag behind. Just as they reached the road one of the calves went down in the shallow ditch there. The other calf stood in the road with his mother and they waited for him. Finally, the mother walked back and bent her head to him. She talked to him and he tried. We saw him try to struggle to his feet, but he was through.

There wasn't much time left for them. The fire was creeping swiftly up the hill and smoke was drifting across the road. A cow moose will sacrifice her life for her calves and I knew the agony and despair in her as she walked away from one calf and took the other with her into the deep woods on the far side of the road. She would try to find a safe place for him at least.

I got out of the car and walked to the ditch and picked the calf up. He was as limp as a rag. He was probably two months old and may have weighed thirty pounds. Most of him was just four long legs. I went round to Ann's side of the car and she opened her door and I laid him on her lap. Time was getting short for us, too, for the fire was close to the road now. I turned the car around and we drove down the hill to the highway.

Before we reached home the calf was sound asleep in Ann's lap. I carried him inside the house and we went to Frank's room. Frank was sleeping and his bed was big enough for both of them, so we pulled the bedclothes back and moved the little fellow close to Frank's side, his head on the pillow. His coat was still damp from fear and exhaustion and he needed the warmth that Frank could give him. We covered them up. Frank was still sound asleep.

Frank's reaction the next morning was a shock of amazement and then accusation. He came into our room and spoke in a whisper.

"There's a moose in my bed. He's a calf."

"Well, when we brought him home last night he was a tired little guy. There was a fire on the West Hill road. When we found him, he just couldn't go any more."

"You should have waked me up—I might have rolled over on him. Next time, you wake me up."

Ann took one of Cathy's old milk bottles and filled it with a rich mixture of evaporated milk and a small amount of water. She added a little corn syrup and put the nipple on it. The calf was still sleeping when I picked him up and took him to the living room. The carpet there was thick and soft and his small hoofs wouldn't slip or slide. He went after his bottle of milk and when he'd finished he nudged Ann; she was his mother now and he wanted more. It was no good being sentimental, though. I called the Department of Game and they came and took him away. They maintained a place above Palmer specially for strays like him.

10 / *Earthquake and Moose Murder*

On March 27, 1964, it was Good Friday.

I always drove a company truck home after work. I kept it there, for two or three times each week I'd get phone calls at night to say someone was without electricity. It was part of my job to take care of that.

Frank and John used to stay after school and practice basketball or baseball. They always waited by the road in front of the schoolhouse, for they knew I'd be there about 5:30 to pick them up.

That afternoon we were part of the way home. The time was 5:36.

"Dad, the snow's falling off the tops of the trees."

"There's probably a high wind up there, Frank."

I was having difficulty keeping the truck straight on the road. I felt as though I was shaking, and thinking there might be something wrong with me, I stopped the truck. I opened the door and stepped to the ground and to keep from falling down I had to grab the door and hang on. I knew what it was now. A giant hand had the earth in its grasp, and the earth was shaking.

I climbed back into the truck and we waited. The wheels on one side rose a foot in the air and slammed down again. The violence increased in force and for a time I thought the truck might turn over. It was almost five minutes before the earth was still, but it seemed much longer to us.

When we got home, I ran to the house.

"Ann, are you all right? Is anything damaged?"

"There's a broken water pipe down in the basement."

I ran down there and shut the valve off and hurried back upstairs.

"Ann, I've got to go. I don't know when I'll be home."

I didn't get home again for three days. Power line poles had been snapped off and crossarms broken, wires were down everywhere. We didn't repair the lines; there was too much damage for that. We simply patched things together and got power back to the people.

A few old houses in Homer had tumbled to the ground but there were no large buildings to collapse, so the damage was minor and no one was injured. The Homer Spit, and all the coastline of the Kenai Peninsula, sank eight feet, but Cook Inlet and Kachemak Bay protected us from the great tidal waves that devastated every town and village along the outer coast and the Aleutian Islands.

Spring was coming to Alaska and the temperature was rising. People were already betting on when the ice breakup would come on the Nenana river. Betting on the Nenana breakup was an annual event and the lucky winner could win from fifty to a hundred thousand dollars.

Deep down under the earth's crust, in an eternal darkness without seasons, a huge layer of boiling pitchlike substance rings the great iron core of the planet. This huge mass of substance wears and strains at the earth's crust and where the crust is weak it may crack. Alaska is known to lie on a relatively weak layer of crust and is subject to many small tremors and quakes.

On that Good Friday, across more than six hundred miles of mountains and towns, forests and icy streams, across great expanses of snow broken only by animal tracks, the earth strained and groaned and shook. In untold hundreds of places it cracked open and in hundreds of places it buckled and toppled buildings, swayed trees and poles in wild arcs, heaved up pavements, snapped bridges and sheared avalanches of snow and dirt and stone from mountaintops, and out in the sea it raised mighty waves. Ground in an area of perhaps a hundred and ten thousand square miles was elevated or depressed by the violent disruption of the earth. Ground in many places rose by more than six feet and in some by more than thirty. Beaches and docks were left high and dry in those areas that rose; homes, the seashore and forests were submerged and destroyed in those areas that dropped.

Anchorage, Alaska's largest city, rests on top of a shelf of clay. Under violent stress, such as the shock waves produced by a violent earthquake, this structure of clay assumes the consistency of jelly. Many homes and business buildings, especially on the west side of the city, simply sank out of sight.

The quake of March 27, 1964, caused greater deformation of the earth's crust than any recorded earthquake before or since. According to the Richter Scale, the San Francisco quake of 1906 registered 7.9, that of 1989 reached 7.1. The Alaska shock of 1964 was recorded at 9.2. The practical top of the scale is 9.5 . . .

The deaths caused by the greatest earthquake in North American history totaled only a hundred and twenty-five. Loss of life was incredibly low, a fact some explained in terms of Alaska's sparse population, its small towns, its broad streets and low buildings; others found the answer on their knees.

The Denali Theater on Fourth Avenue in Anchorage was showing a late afternoon matinée for children. At 5:36 the building began to shake and the lights went out. The dim emergency lights came on and the manager ran down the center aisle.

"You kids stay in your seats! Don't you move!" he shouted.

It was as though the theater was on an elevator. It sank fifteen feet straight down into the ground and five hundred kids stayed in their seats. After the building stopped shaking, the manager showed all the children how to climb out to safety. Not one of them was injured. All the buildings around were piles of broken concrete rubble but that portion of the Denali that still showed above ground was standing firm.

The highest death toll was in Valdez. There, thirty-one men, women and children who were standing on the dock watching the freighter *Chena* unload her cargo were swept away by the giant wave that destroyed the town.

The *Chena* rose about thirty feet, then dropped. It rose again, and dropped. The third time the water rose she was pointing toward the open sea. By then the ship was under way and could move to deep water and safety. Two men on the ship were killed by falling cargo and another died of a heart attack.

Far to the southwest, in Kodiak Harbor, Bill Cuthbert, an old-time fisherman, was sitting down to supper in the galley of his eighty-six-foot fishing boat, the *Selief*. In the hold were three thousand dollars' worth of Alaskan king crabs ready to be unloaded next morning at the cannery.

The first tidal wave was gentle, a gradual swell followed by a gradual ebb. The second wave hit with a roar and in a few seconds every piling, every anchor, every line and every pier snapped and broke and the harbor became a dizzy whirlpool.

State Trooper Don Church had the entire Aleutian chain as his district. After the first tidal wave hit Kodiak, he rushed to the police station to sound the alarm over the marine radio, trying to contact each of the remote tiny villages. Some of them showed on the maps, others only in the trooper's notebook. Village by village, he tried them all, then he began contacting fishing boats. Most of them replied but for some the warning came too late.

Bill Cuthbert on the *Selief* heard the warning.

"*Selief, Selief,* can you hear me? *Selief,* where are you?"

"It looks," answered Cuthbert, "as though I'm behind the Kodiak schoolhouse, about six blocks from the waterfront." The *Selief* had sailed over trees and houses and between buildings and finally come to rest, right side up.

Chenega was a small fishing village on the shore of Prince William Sound. Within minutes of the first great quake, seismic sea waves surged in and swept Chenega from the face of the earth. Of the seventy-six people who lived there, twenty-three perished. Those who survived were swept into the hills and they climbed higher for safety.

Tina Vlasoff was still in what had been the village after the second wave hit. Her arms were clasped hard round a wooden cross in the graveyard. Her body had been stripped bare by the raging waters but she had a sock on one foot. She saw the third tidal wave coming and she tightened her grip round the cross. She flattened her body to the ground, buried her face in her arms, and she prayed. For Tina, it was a time of terrible fear and yet, perhaps, a time of grace, for she survived.

Property damage in the earthquake was estimated at three billion dollars. Before the Good Friday earthquake, the economy of Seward had been based mainly on shipping. Freighters and oil tankers docked regularly in the harbor and most of their freight was then transported to other parts of Alaska via the Alaskan Railroad and the Seward Highway. Texaco and Standard Oil Company had established huge tank farms on the waterfront.

The entire economy of the town was wiped out by the total destruction of harbor facilities and railroad yards during the quake. The rails themselves were like twisted spaghetti. A diesel locomotive was hurled a hundred yards from the tracks. The huge oil tanks ruptured and the oil burst into flames. The sixty-foot tidal waves lashing the shore were red from raging fires. The Seward area dropped three and a half feet and in the midst of all of this savage destruction, only thirteen people perished.

If Good Friday was for many a time of violence and terror and death, in Anchorage there was one small touch of unintentional humor.

A lady tourist visiting Hewitt's Drug Store downtown showed signs of fear when the first small quake rattled cameras and other things in the glass cases. The clerk behind the counter assured her that there was nothing to be concerned about. "We have small earthquakes all the time."

The next thing the clerk knew he was knocked to the floor behind the counter and the repeated tremors had shaken most of the stock off the shelves and left the store in a shambles. When he was able to stand he looked over the top of the counter and found his customer just getting to her feet. She brushed off her clothes and said, "My goodness, I don't see how you people put up with this all the time."

❋   ❋   ❋

I believe the Kenai Peninsula contained the largest moose herds of any place on earth. They spent the summer months deep in the Caribou Hills and about the first of November, when the deep snows came, they moved down to the low-lands, close to the towns and all over the countryside. This had been their winter home long before there were any people living here. At that time of year they seemed to have no fear of people. I've seen them feeding from haystacks in farmers' fields. On the outskirts of Homer, at times, they could be seen standing in people's yards.

A school bus picked up our three kids in the morning and in the afternoon stopped by our house to let them off again. I don't know how many times they stood by the road and hollered for their mother: moose were standing in the driveway and they wanted her to come and shoo them away. Ann always watched for the school bus to stop and she would come out of the front door with a smile on her face and a broom in her hand. I don't know of one instance when a moose caused any harm.

In 1964 the Department of Game embarked on a program that was unnecessary and a disgrace. They decided that there were too many cow moose for the number of bulls available, so they waited until the moose were down from the hills then declared open season on antlerless moose. The season would run from November 23 to 30. Eight long days of slaughter, mostly of cows and small calves.

Most of the men who regularly hunted moose in the fall were outraged. I talked with a game warden who had been with the department for many years.

"Fred, I know it's wrong but what in hell can I do?"

People came down in droves from Anchorage. Most of them had never in their lives shot a moose. They weren't hunters. This new ruling made things easy for them.

I went to the department's office in Homer and talked to one of their biologists. He had it all cut and dried.

"Any time you have more than ten cows to one bull, some cows may not get bred. Others may be bred late and have late calves, which means a low survival rate for those calves that winter."

He was a biologist, which meant, of course, that he had to be an expert, but he had forgotten some things. Half the calves that were killed that November were little bulls. Even if they weren't shot, every time a cow is killed, two calves die, for most cows have twins. Calves have no chance to make it through the winter without their mother. They need her to break trail for them through the deep snow. They need her at night, when it may be twenty below, to snuggle up to and keep warm.

If a man and his wife had three children who were old enough to hunt, they were entitled to five moose. It wasn't long before the town dump in Homer was littered with hindquarters of moose meat. One day I saw a pickup piled high with calves. I knew the man standing by it and I stopped the truck I was driving and went to him.

"Ernie, why did you do this?"

"I didn't kill all of them, Fred. The guys haven't come out of the woods yet."

"But, Ernie, all you have there is a pile of bone and hair. The little bit of meat on them is flaccid and stringy. You can't eat it."

"But, Fred, it's legal."

"Yes, Ernie, I know. It's legal." As the biologist had told me, late calves might not make it through the winter.

During the antlerless moose season, women who had never had a rifle to their shoulder shot cow moose. Kids who were big enough to hold and aim a rifle shot them. I won't even try to guess how many moose were shot through the stomach and ran off into the heavy brush. A moose shot that way will run for quite a distance, and then it will lie down. It takes a long time to die that way.

I remember a sad thing I saw, the first winter of the cow moose kill. I used to snowshoe up Anchor River and go ptarmigan hunting. One day I saw a flock of ravens ahead of me. They were working on something and they flew off as I got close to them. It was a moose calf and they had plucked out his eyes. They had managed to get holes into his stomach and his intestines were bulging out. He was starving but still alive. I shot him and turned around and went home. Someone had killed his mother.

The Department of Game maintained its antlerless moose cull for two years. The third year they decided there were now too many bulls for the number of cows, so they declared open season on bulls. That meant snow machines. A bull moose would be driven through the deep snow until he couldn't go any more, and then he was shot.

A bull moose, dressed out and delivered to your house—after dark, of course—could be bought for fifty dollars. I know this, for I was approached. The man who tried to sell me a moose made a full-time job of it as long as the season lasted. For several years after the moose were cleaned out, I had to hire a plane to fly me back in the hills; if I stayed out a week, I could manage to find a bull for our winter supply. The moose will come back again if they are left alone. I believe public outcry these days would prevent there ever being another antlerless moose season on the Kenai.

11 / *A Lonely Time*

Homer was a place that grew slowly. No one came there to get rich, it wasn't that kind of town. Every summer a few people found their way there. Some of them liked what they saw, and they stayed.

Jack Scott owned a grocery store. He decided Homer was big enough to support a bowling alley and he converted his store. He had to add on to the back of it to make it longer, but he was determined to have a bowling alley. I think at one time Jack had lived where he'd done quite a bit of bowling, for after his new place opened he seemed to be pretty proficient.

There was plenty of recreation around Homer but this was the first thing that offered competition. I believe teams were formed even before the alley was ready. Everyone in town was determined to be a bowler. The way it turned out, we all learned how to bowl. As time went on we all improved but some of us became really good, and some of us developed into experts.

Ann was one of the experts. She went to every bowling tournament in Alaska—Fairbanks, Kodiak, Anchorage, she went to them all. She had trophies that said she had won the Women's Singles Championship in three tournaments. One Saturday, in April 1972, we learned there was to be a bowling tournament in Seward. I wasn't surprised when Ann told me she'd like to go.

"That's a two-hundred-mile drive, honey."

"The tournament starts at nine-thirty. We can leave here early."

We left at five in the morning and Cathy went with us. We arrived in Seward around nine o'clock and by the time we had our bowling shoes on it was time for the tournament to open. There was a pinball game there, a partition separating it from the alleys. I gave Cathy enough quarters to keep her busy, then Ann and I took our places.

I had thrown two balls and I had a real feeling that something was wrong. I looked over to where Ann was bowling and I saw her as she reached for the scoring table with her hand. She fell to the floor.

I ran to her. She was lying on her back, gasping for breath and trying to breathe, and then she stopped. I knelt by her and I gave her mouth-to-mouth resuscitation and depressed her heart with the palms of my hands. The ambulance came and they placed an oxygen mask over her face. I kept it in place as they put her in the ambulance and we rode to the hospital.

They laid Ann on a table in the emergency room, and a nurse put in place the small wires that led to the electrocardiograph. The doctor was depressing her heart with his hands, and I watched the straight line. The only time it was broken was when he applied pressure. He tried for a long time. Then I heard him say, "I'm sorry."

I turned to him and he said, "She was gone before we got her here. There was no chance at all."

I looked at Ann. I think I almost thought she might waken.

If there is unbearable, never-ending pain, death may come as a gentle gift. Ann had been so filled with life and happiness, it was wrong that she was like this. So quiet, and so still.

"Had your wife been having a heart problem?"

"No. There was nothing."

I bent to Ann and kissed her forehead, and I left.

A patrol car was waiting for me and they drove me back to the bowling hall. All our friends were waiting for me as I went in, and I shook my head. Other than a feeling of terrible loss, my mind was empty of any emotion and I don't know why I went to the woman behind the counter. She took care of tournament fees and other things that go with bowling.

"How can I tell a little girl her mother is dead?"

I saw the hopeless look on her face and she said, "I don't know."

I turned away and saw Cathy. She was still playing the pinball game, unaware that anything had happened. I walked over.

"Cathy, we're going home now."

"All right, Daddy."

We went outside and got in the car and I started the motor.

"Where's Mamma?"

There's no easy way to answer a question like that. When I told her, Cathy looked at me then turned away and stared out of the window.

I backed the car out onto the highway and we drove away. The miles home were the longest miles of my life, for not once did Cathy turn to me. It wasn't till we reached home that she came to me and hung on. She cried then, for a long time. I never saw her cry again. She may have, in her room at night, when she was alone.

Frank was eighteen and in his last year at high school. He telephoned his brother and sisters and they were all there the next day. Frank took care of everything for me. He had friends with equipment that could break the frozen earth and he had friends who helped him dig his mother's grave.

I drove to the cemetery the next day to see if he was all right. He was standing down in Ann's grave with a shovel in his hands, smoothing the sides, very carefully. I didn't let him know I was there. I drove away.

On the day of Ann's funeral, the stores in town closed. The church was filled with her friends and more of them were standing outside. After the service we drove to the cemetery and Frank and John and I helped carry the casket, for this was our task. The day was cold and snow was blowing across the side of the hill. One of our friends had Cathy folded in his overcoat, in front of him.

I looked at her and saw the pleading in her eyes. I knew Ann wouldn't want this. I couldn't let Cathy hurt any more and I went to her.

"Let's go home."

"Daddy, where is Mamma?"

"She's here with us, Cathy. She'll always be with us."

I looked at her small, sad face and it showed a ray of hope.

"You know, Cathy, whenever you need your mother, she'll be with you."

We drove home and went into our house. It seemed empty and I was glad when the rest of the kids got home. That night, after everyone was in bed, I sat in a big easy chair in the living room and tried to go over things in my mind. John would be going back to his work in Anchorage. The three older girls would be leaving for their homes in the outside States. Frank planned to go to the University of Hawaii in the fall. That would leave Cathy and me.

The house was quiet. I got up and walked softly down the hall. Patty was in Cathy's bed. I went on to our room, and in the dim light of a small bedside lamp I saw Cathy. She was curled up with a photograph of her mother hugged to her breast. I left her and walked to Frank's room. I could hear a slight sound and went to his bedside. He was crying in his sleep. I reached down and touched him gently on his shoulder, and went back to my chair.

There is a saying that you can start your life over every day you live. It wasn't going to be that easy for me.

I remembered the time, so long ago, when I had asked Ann if she would marry me.

"Ann, will you marry me and go to that big lake country with me?"

"Fred, I will. I'll marry you and I'll go wherever you go."

Ann was only forty-nine when she died. I wish she could have stayed with me but it was like wishing on a star. If you're lucky, a little bit of stardust might fall. Maybe it did that night, for as I sat there I knew I heard Ann's voice.

"Don't worry, Fred, everything is all right."

❊   ❊   ❊

In two more days everyone was gone except Frank, Cathy and me. Cathy's birthday was on May 4. She was ten years old. Not many days after that, Frank came to me.

"Dad, I'll be graduating before long. Would it be okay if I leave for Hawaii then? I can see what things are like there and find some kind of job. I'll be ready for school this fall."

For the first time I realized he was really going to leave, and Hawaii was a long way away.

I had taught him how to use a fly rod for trout: "Always cast your fly upstream and let it drift down slow and easy. Hold the tip of your rod up, so that the fly floats on the surface. Always let your fly drift into every little eddy, for that's where the trout will be lying, and then you'll get a strike." I had taken him moose hunting with me and I'd taught him how to call a bull: "When you can call a moose this way, it's a lot better than beating through the brush looking for one."

He left the first week in June. Cathy and I went with him to the airport and we had some time before his flight took off. We talked about everything except his leaving us. I told him he'd enjoy a new place like Hawaii. He said he'd write to us. Then it really was time for him to leave, and he hugged us both.

"Cathy, you be a good girl and take care of Dad."

We watched him as he climbed the steps leading to the door of the plane. He turned and waved and he was gone.

I wished he hadn't had to go.

❄ ❄ ❄

Our living room had four big picture windows, one on each end and two facing the road out front. We had a couch by the window at the north end where Cathy and I used to sit late at night. At five minutes past eleven a satellite would rise above the horizon in the northwest. The time never varied, not one minute either way. It looked like a huge, beautiful star. It took it perhaps two full minutes to sail in slow majesty across the night sky and disappear on the horizon in the southeast.

Cathy and I were watching it one night when she turned to me.

"Daddy, wouldn't you like to go somewhere?"

I was sixty-two years old and I had taken early retirement after Ann's death. Cathy and I could go almost anywhere we wanted to.

"I know what we'll do, Cathy. We'll sell our house and we'll fly to Seattle. We'll buy a car there and we'll be just like that satellite. We'll go everywhere."

❄ ❄ ❄

It was June. Cathy and I were standing together in the vestibule of St. Mary's Chapel.

Two years before, in 1981, she had graduated from West High School in Charlotte, North Carolina. Cathy looked a lot like her mother. She was a beautiful girl and she was in her wedding gown.

St. Mary's Chapel was well over a hundred years old and it was used now just for weddings. We heard the organ music and Cathy put her arm through mine and I walked with her down the aisle, and we stopped in front of the altar. I gave Cathy away and she became Mrs. Michael Rogers.

I was seventy-three years old now and didn't plan to attend the after-wedding festivities. I stood outside the chapel and watched the wedding party get into their cars. Cathy and Michael came out and I saw her looking for me. She saw me and came flying and threw her arms around me and hugged me.

"Daddy, I love you."

Cathy would be leaving me now, and I knew the feeling of being just a little lonely.

12 / *The Big Lake Country*

I ARRIVED IN ANCHORAGE LATE THE NEXT DAY and spent that night in the Westward Hotel. I boarded the plane for Homer the next morning.

Cathy and I had left Homer eleven years before and it had grown. There was a car rental agency at the airport now. I rented a car and drove up West Hill to the cemetery. I walked to Ann's grave and knelt there, pulling at the small grass that was growing. I took my handkerchief and rubbed the bronze marker until it was bright and clear, and read the words:

Ann Hatfield, 1923–1972
Beloved Wife of Fred

"Honey, I'm going back to our little lake in the Tikchiks. You and I lived there together for a long time and I know I'll find you there. The kids turned out fine, and we all love you."

I drove back to the airport and waited for the plane to take me back to Anchorage. Next morning I boarded a plane and we flew west, toward Bristol Bay.

We circled over Dillingham before we landed. It was difficult to believe the changes that had taken place. What had been a small village thirty years before was a good-sized town now. Gravel roads ran for a long way in every direction. The waterfront was a solid line of buildings; I found out later they were freezer plants for salmon.

We landed and I walked to the flight office of Dillingham Air Service. I sat down there for a while. I hadn't heard from anyone in Bristol Bay for a long time and I wasn't sure there would be anyone left that I used to know. I walked to the counter and spoke to the girl there.

"Do you know a man named Orville Braswell?"

"Everyone knows Orville."

"If he has a phone, would you see if you can reach him?"

She dialed a number and handed me the phone. A woman's voice said, "Hello?"

"I'm Fred Hatfield. Is Orville home?"

"He's out back somewhere. Are you the man who used to live in the Tikchiks?"

"Yes, I'm the one. I'm at the airfield."

"I'll be right out to pick you up."

That had been Alice talking to me. She had married Orville about the same time Ann and I were married. I sat down and waited and it wasn't long before a pickup stopped in front of the office. I went outside. After thirty years I still recognized her, and I hugged her.

"How's Orville?"

"He's just the same, Fred. Older, like we are."

They still lived in the house Orville had built forty years ago.

"You'll find Orville out back in one of the sheds. He's probably hanging floats on a gill net."

I went around behind the house and heard sounds in one of the buildings. I found Orville and we shook hands. It had been a long time.

"Fred, I never expected to see you again."

"I wasn't sure I'd find anyone left."

"There aren't many. Let's go to the house."

We sat at the kitchen table.

"So how many of us are there?"

"Half of us are sitting right here, Fred. You and me. The other half are Matt Flenzburg and Red Tilton. How old are you, Fred?"

"I'm seventy-three."

"That makes you the youngest. I'm seventy-six and so is Red. Matt Flenzburg is eighty. What in the world are you back in this country for?"

"There are two things I want to do. I want to fly into Togiak Lake and see if there's some place a plane can land close to the creek I found in that high pass, the creek that's supposed to be half gold."

"Fred, you don't give up easy."

"It isn't that. I just don't have many things left to do. I want to fly into the Tikchiks. I'd like to spend a night on the little lake where Patty was born."

Orville looked at me and nodded his head.

"You're in luck. I have a son, Leon. He's a commercial pilot and has his own plane. He'll take you wherever you want to go, and I'd like to ride along with you."

"You'll have to find a piece of canvas for me, Orville, big enough for a lean-to shelter. I'll need two or three blankets and an axe, and you'll have to lend me your rifle."

We left for Togiak Lake the next morning. We flew over the lake and into the pass. I pointed out the creek to Leon and he flew for two miles in every direction, trying to find a ridgetop smooth enough for wheels, or a small lake close enough to land on with floats, but there was nothing.

"You need a chopper for that creek, Fred. That could set you down right where you need to be."

"Maybe next year."

We passed over a range of mountains and flew the length of the third lake. It's the largest of the Tikchiks, over forty-five miles long. I had taken lake trout from it that were almost as long as I was.

Finally, Leon set his plane down on a good-sized river. He wasn't too far above the head of a set of rapids and I saw that the plane was drifting backwards in the swift current. I tapped him on the shoulder.

"Leon, if you let your plane get into those rapids you won't get out. They don't look too good."

He laughed and gunned the motor and we rose from the water. Orville turned to me.

"Fred, do you know where we are?"

"No, I sure don't."

"This is the Nuyakuk river. Remember the year you found John Shipton running wild at Rat Lake? You brought him down all these rivers and took him out to the coast. You ran those rapids in a canoe."

"They didn't look that bad then."

"The rapids haven't changed, Fred. You have. That was about forty-five years ago."

We flew north and in a while we were over a small lake, a lake I knew. It was joined to another, smaller lake by a narrow run of water.

"Is this where you and Ann lived, Fred?"

I nodded. "This is where Patty was born."

Leon cut the throttle and circled low round the lake, and I saw it. It was as though our cabin had waited for us to come back and we never did. It had collapsed all at once, for the split roof logs were lying on the ground side by side, so nice and straight. I could almost see our kids playing on the lake shore, and Ann in the yard. There should have been a sturdy cabin there, standing strong and defiant.

The high mountains, the wide deep valleys and the wild rivers, they don't change. Manmade things and man himself change, and after a time there is nothing.

Leon pointed down. Below us and close to the old cabin site were two grizzlies. One of them was huge and had a silver streak a foot wide running the length of his back.

"Land close to the old cabin, will you?"

All of us climbed out and Leon made his plane fast to shore.

"You know, Orville, with those grizzlies around I'll need a fire going full time. They don't like smoke. You and Leon will have to help me get plenty of wood together."

Orville and I didn't gather much wood but Leon stacked up more than enough. They helped me get my lean-to shelter in shape and a good fire going. I had Orville's rifle and the blankets and an axe.

"Fred, I'll be in to pick you up first thing in the morning."

"There's no hurry. Any time tomorrow will be fine."

They left then and I walked to where our cabin had been.

It was difficult to realize that no one had been there since Ann and I and the kids had left, a long time ago. Everything looked lonely and desolate now. I saw a small, thin shell of rust on the ground. I picked it up and it fell to pieces in my hand. At one time it had been part of our stove. There was nothing else left. I walked back to my fire and sat there for a while. I carried my rifle and walked the lake shore, to the small gut of water. The stones that Ann and I had used for our whitefish trap were still there in a neat pile and I placed a line of them across the water. I sat down then and waited for the fish to come. They hadn't changed. They still circled the lakes, from right to left. They entered my trap and I fenced them off. I flipped three of them out of the water and replaced the stones, back where I'd found them, nice and neat.

I cleaned my fish and raked a pile of coals from the fire. I covered the fish with the coals and in fifteen minutes they were done.

Darkness was almost here now and I found a soft place on the lake shore and sat. A cow moose and her two calves emerged from the willows and began to feed on the tender growth by the water.

Across the lake I could see the outline of the hill against the night sky, the hill that Ann and I had climbed together so many times.

I heard the far-off cry of wolves. They had smelled the smoke from the fire, and I knew they would come.

The grizzlies had heard the cry and they would be moving slowly away.

The moose would take her calves and find a thick growth of willows. She would lie there and be very quiet.

There was complete silence now, for every living thing in that land had the utmost respect for a wolf pack.

In an incredibly short time they were there. The beginning of a wolf's lonely, beautiful song announced their presence.

I remembered the time that Ann and I had been sitting here, and the wolves had come.

"Fred, are the wolves as lonely as they sound?"

Their song tonight was the same beautiful thing it had been then. From somewhere deep in their throats it has its beginning, very low. It rises in pitch, ever higher, until it is lost in silence. Each seemed to take a turn, in the wild song of the wolf.

Finally it was over and they were leaving. They had finished their inspection of the strange smell of smoke and they were going back where they'd come from. The silence they had imposed would endure for some time yet.

Just being there brought back so many wonderful little things Ann and I had shared together, and I knew now why I had felt the strong desire to return once more. Wherever I had walked today Ann had been walking with me, and the quiet of the night gave me a feeling of peace. Memories fill the pages of time and it's almost as though you were living life over again. The love and faith Ann and I had shared would never go away, for they were safe in my mind and heart and nothing, not even time, could take them from me.

I rose to my feet and went to the dying fire and laid the rest of the wood across it. There was enough to last until morning. I went to the lean-to, rolled the blankets around me, and slept.

I woke to the sound of Leon's plane. He was early, for the sun had just tipped the horizon.

He pulled his plane in close and stepped out.

"What kind of night did you have?"

"It was a fine, wonderful night."

We took the rifle and axe and the blankets and folded the canvas I had used for shelter. We climbed on board and Leon taxied to the end of the lake. He revved his motor, the plane gained speed and we lifted from the water. He put the plane into a sharp bank, then leveled off and headed for the coast.

What I had gone there to find was with me now, and I didn't look back.